DEMOCRATIC PROCESSES IN CENTRAL ASIA

Indo-Kazakh Perspectives

DEMOCRATIC PROCESSES IN CENTRAL ASIA

Indo-Kazakh Perspectives

Editors:

K. Santhanam

Baizakova Kuralay Irtysovna

Kukeyeva Fatima Turarovna

THE INDIA-CENTRAL ASIA FOUNDATION

New Delhi

AL-FARABI KAZAKH NATIONAL UNIVERSITY

Almaty

INDIAN COUNCIL OF WORLD AFFAIRS

New Delhi

ARYAN BOOKS INTERNATIONAL

New Delhi

DEMOCRATIC PROCESSES IN CENTRAL ASIA:
INDO-KAZAKH PERSPECTIVES

ISBN: 978-81-7305-371-9

Published in **2009** by:

THE INDIA-CENTRAL ASIA FOUNDATION
C9/9872, Vasant Kunj, New Delhi-110 070

AL-FARABI KAZAKH NATIONAL UNIVERSITY
Almaty

INDIAN COUNCIL OF WORLD AFFAIRS
Sapru House, Barakhamba Road, New Delhi

and

ARYAN BOOKS INTERNATIONAL
Pooja Apartments, 4B, Ansari Road, New Delhi - 110 002 (India)
Tel.: 23287589, 23255799; Fax: 91-11-23270385
E-mail: aryanbooks@vsnl.com, aryanbooks@gmail.com

Computer Typeset and Printed in India at
ABI Prints & Publishing Co., New Delhi

Preface

GENERAL

One of the distinctive features of the present world order is the growing significance of Asia, particularly Eurasia, in international politics. Central Asian region has drawn considerable external attention mainly because of its location in the center of Eurasia and its abundant raw materials, especially energy resources. A parallel development is the emergence of India as a major regional power. India's rising profile, its economic prowess and growing strategic interests necessitate that the Central Asian region remain stable, democratic and secular. The Central Asian States perceive India to be a friendly and a dependable country. They desire to learn from India's experience in politico-social-economic development as well. At the regional level Kazakhstan has emerged as a leading country. Its vast energy resources and skillful utilization of this resource has enabled it to emerge as a leading player in the Central Asian region. India and Kazakhstan share compatible interests on various issues of international concerns such as terrorism, extremism, drug trafficking, etc. Indian experience in building democratic institutions could be useful to Kazakhstan. A significant milestone in the relationship was the Declaration of Strategic Partnership signed during President Nursultan Nazarbayev's visit to India during January 23-26, 09. It reflects a qualitative change in the relations between the two countries.

In the twenty-first century, increased cooperation between Kazakhstan and India assumes a higher relevance. There are areas of cooperation of mutual benefit. We believe that the potential to gainfully contribute to the shaping of events in Central Asia and contiguous regions is high and deserves to be pursued in a sustained manner.

Kazakhstan's geopolitical position at the juncture of Asia and Europe, its economic and military-political interests, and its existing economic potential ensures the country's place in the system of modern international relations as a regional power actively working towards, a zone of good-neighbourliness based on the principle of equal security. Kazakhstan's foreign policy is based on a multi vector approach; friendship towards all countries. In 2010 Kazkahstan would take over as the Chairman of the Organisation for Cooperation and Security in Europe (OSCE).

Kazakhstan is deeply engaged in the process of nation building after the dawn of independence in 1991. Rarely has history witnessed a unique event like the simultaneous emergence of an independent state and involved in the process of a systemic transition. How soon and successfully the transition is completed is of considerable interest to the international community in general and to neighbours in particular. In pursuing policies for a successful transformation every nation would have to take care and see that its policies are in harmony with their respective traditions, value system and culture. Democratic process is an evolutionary one. Its pace cannot be shortened nor can it be quickened. The Central Asian States stand to benefit from other countries experience particularly from that of India.

It is against this backdrop that ICAF felt the need for scholarly exchanges with Kazakhstan on matters of common interest. This joint study has taken the shape of the book after months of planning, discussions and exchanges with the Department of International Relations of the Al-Farabi Kazakh National University, Almaty.

COVERAGE OF TOPICS

This volume is a collection of 17 papers written by scholars from Kazakhstan and India, the authors strived to show the process of democratization in Central Asia in general and Kazakhstan in particular and the entire gamut of issues mentioned above.

Dr. Anita Sengupta provides in depth analysis of various definitions of Eurasia in the context of current political realities in Kazakhstan. She underlines on the alternative Kazakh definitions of Eurasia which assumes significance to the extent that it challenges the essentializing and exceptionalist rhetoric of nationalist politics. She is of the view that understanding of Eurasia will determine the contours of contemporary Kazakh politics.

Prof. Baizakova's paper focuses on the presidential system in Kazakhstan and its role in promoting democratic processes in social, political and economic spheres. She believes that transition to democracy is not a linear process. It is rather a very long and difficult process which may be fraught with serious threats to the socio-political development of the country. She underlines the fact that the political reforms in Kazakhstan are being carried out by the state itself without destabilizing the society.

Prof. Umarov's contribution provides an analysis of the current trend of democratisation in Central Asia countries. He underlines that the state structure of these countries has undergone fundamental changes in comparison with what existed during the Soviet times. He states that sincere attempts were made to change the single-party system during Soviet time also. However, dismantling of the Soviet Union led to a pluralist, multi-party political system in Kazakhstan, Kyrgyzstan and Tajikistan. Turkmenistan and Uzbekistan followed the route of controlled democratisation.

Rustam Burnashev and Irina Chernykh's contribution is focussed on the idea of democracy and liberal values within the framework of identity and pluralist societies in Central Asia in general and Uzbekistan in particular. They underline that the formation of identity necessarily implies identification of one or more of *Others.* They argue that identification of *Others* helps in 'constructing' the identity from security point of view.

K.N. Makasheva's contribution critically examines Russian and American policies towards democratic processes in Kazakhstan while highlighting local conditions for development of democracy there. She underlines that India and Kazakhstan both being multi-religious and multi-ethnic countries have common interest at regional and international levels. She has argued for enhance role of New Delhi in Central Asia and international affairs.

Galiev's paper has focussed on the revived and invented traditions in the political systems of Kazakhstan, Kyrgyzstan, Tajikistan, Turkmenistan and Uzbekistan. He underlines the importance of traditional political systems of the Central Asian countries in today's context.

G.A. Urozbaeva's paper provides an indepth analysis of the traditional legal institutions of the nomads of Eurasia. She argues that traditional legal institutions and historically developed norms of the common law were an inseparable part of the spiritual culture of the nomads of Eurasia. She is of the view that development of democratic norms and revival of the national culture are taking place simultaneously in Kazakhstan and Kalmykiya (Russia). She underlines that revival of any of the traditional legal institutions requires a more careful approach, and in so doing the existing realities of modern life have to be taken into consideration along with the possibilities of adjustment of the 'revived' traditions within the modern legal system.

Fatima Kukeyeva critically examines the issue of democratization in Central Asia and the US foreign policy strategy in the region. She believes that the US needs to balance its geopolitical and economic interests with the desire of Central Asian peoples to obtain democracy. She further explains role of the internal and external dynamics in democratic reforms in Central Asian countries.

M.Sh. Gubaidullina's contribution stresses on the role of Organisation for security and Cooperation in Europe (OSCE) and European Union (EU) in the political reforms/transformation in Kazakhstan today. She believes that any discussion of the current political process in Kazakhstan should be with in the framework of the declaration "On Sovereignty" and the Constitutional Act "On State Independence of the Republic of Kazakhstan". Both the documents mention the necessity to create a legitimate State, the first one puts emphasis on "democracy" and the second one – on "civil society". She underlines that these documents signify beginning of the formation of a new system of political rule, institutions, directions and values of society.

Sapanov's paper examines the evolving democratic system in Kazakhstan based on the constitutional principles. He underlines that democratic reforms and transformation process in Kazakhstan have been able to avoid political crises which could have led to destabilization of the society. He underlines that Kazakh Presidential form of rule is based on French mode. He further dwells on the history of evolution of Presidential form of governance in Kazakhstan.

P.L. Dash's paper examines problems faced in advancing democratic reforms in Central Asia in general and Uzbekistan in particular. He believes that political elites in Central Asian countries are themselves responsible for either in slowing down democratic process or refusing to give due space to the Opposition. He has selected the case of Turkmenistan for this analysis.

Aliya Askarovna Akataeva makes a comparative analysis of political systems of India and Kazakhstan. She analyses the constitutional system of Kazakhstan and the role of political groups / parties / organizations in ongoing democratic process there. She critically examines the role of political parties in India with in the constitutional framework.

Lessya Karataeva's paper examines the current status and protection of Human Rights in Kazakhstan especially in the context of fighting religious extremism and international terrorism. She articulates Kazakh government position and initiatives in promoting and protecting the Human Rights in that country.

Kuldeep Singh's paper focuses on current economic reforms underway in Central Asia in general and Kazakhstan in particular. R.G. Gidadhubli and Sanjay Deshpande's contribution is focussed on the possibilities and constraints of cooperation between South and Central Asia. They have analysed the availability of resources in Central Asian region and highlighted the need for a southward opening for these countries.

Jyotsna Bakshi's contribution has focussed on regional cooperation between South Asia and Central Asia. She states historical and cultural commonalities between the two regions. She critically analyses double game of Pakistan government towards Central Asia. Issues of religious extremism and transport connectivity remain important factors to enhance cooperation between South and Central Asia, she adds.

N. Kundu in her paper focuses on re-emergence of Taliban and the threats they pose to security and stability in Central and South Asia. She argues for stable, strong and democratic Afghanistan which would be a step forward in promoting democracy and development in Central Asia.

We are happy to offer this volume to scholars, policy makers, diplomats, entrepreneurs, academics and decision makers in both countries as well as those with a similar interest in the democratic processes in Central Asia and foreign policies of India and Kazakhstan.

ACKNOWLEDGEMENTS

We would like to record our appreciation of the support extended by the Indian Council of World Affairs (ICWA), New Delhi. It is a pleasure to say a special word of thanks to Ambassador Ashok Kumar, Director-General, ICWA, New Delhi for his enthusiastic support to the study. Sincere thanks are also due to Dr. Nivedita Das Kundu, Research Fellow, ICWA.

We would like to thank all the authors of papers published in the book. A word of praise is also due to Aliya Askarovna Akataeva, Assistant Professor, Department of International Relations, Al-Farabi Kazakh National University, Almaty and ICAF Research Coordinator in New Delhi for valuable assistance in publication. Without their dedication and persistent hard work, this book may not have seen the light of day.

Sincere thanks are also due to ICAF Governing Body members especially to Amb K. Raghunath, Prof. Nirmala Joshi, Shri J. N. Roy and Brig Devinder Singh and faculty members of the Department of International Relations of the Al-Farabi Kazakh National University for valuable assistance in executing the project.

We would like to record our appreciation of the efforts made by Prof. H.C. Pande for translating the Russian papers and by M/s Aryan Books International for copy-editing and preparing this volume for publication in time despite the inevitable delays.

January 05, 2009

K. Santhanam
New Delhi

K. Baizakova and
Fatima Kukeyeva
Almaty

Contents

About the Editors

K. Santhanam is presently President of The India-Central Asia Foundation (ICAF). He was Director General, Institute for Defence Studies Analyses (IDSA), New Delhi till July 31 2004 and earlier was Chief Adviser (Technology) in the Defence Research and Development Organisation (DRDO). He has worked for about 43 years in the area of science, technology and security and contributed to the evolution of India's positions on disarmament and arms control. He has served as India member in the Inter-Governmental Committee of Experts set up by the UN Secretary General (1978-80) on verification of arms control treaties, has been Scientific Adviser in the Ministry of External affairs (1984-86) and a member of the National Security Advisory Board. He was conferred the *Padma Bhushan* award in recognition of his contributions to the Shakti-98 series of nuclear tests conducted in May 1998. He *was* the editor, *Strategic Analysis* (New Delhi). His published works include co-authorship of *Jihadis in Jammu and Kashmir: A Portrait Gallery* (Sage Publications, New Delhi 2003); *Iraq War 2003: Rise of the New 'Unilateralism'* (Ane Books, New Delhi 2003); *Asian Security and China 2000-2010* (Shipra Publications, New Delhi 2004); *India And Central Asia: Advancing the Common Interest* (IDSA and Anamaya Publishers, New Delhi, 2004); *India And Kazakhstan Relations: Enhancing the Partnership* (KazISS, Almaty and Anamaya Publishers, New Delhi, 2006); *India-Tajikistan Cooperation: Perspectives and Prospects* (ICAF & Anamaya Publishers, New Delhi, 2007); *India-Kazakhstan Perspectives: Regional and International Interactions* (Al-Farabi Kazakh National University, Almaty, ICAF & Anamaya Publishers, New Delhi, 2007); *India-Turkmenistan Relations* (ICAF & Anamaya Publishers, 2007), *Indo-Uzbek*

Perspectives on the Environment and Sustainable Development (ICAF & Anamaya Publishers, 2007) and *Contemporary Indo-Uzbek Perspectives on Bilateral and Regional Issues* (Al-Farabi Kazakh National University, Almaty, ICAF & Anamaya Publishers, New Delhi, 2009).

krishnamurthy.santhanam@gmail.com

Prof. Baizakova Kuralay Irtysovna is currently Dean of the Department of International Relations, Al-Farabi Kazakh National University, Almaty. She is also director of the European Documentation Centre (Al-Farabi KazNU) since 2002 and the chief editor of *European Dialogue* magazine. She is director of the NATO Resource and Information Centre since 2006 at the KazNU. She was honoured with the best supervisor of students' scientific researches by Ministry of Education and Science of the Republic of Kazakhstan. Prof. Baizakova was awarded with the honour of *The best Lecturer of the year 2005* by the Ministry of Education and Science for her contribution in the fields of European and American history, international relations, theory of international relations, problems of regional and national security, international security structures, regional conflicts and their resolution, process of European integration and security problems in Central Asian region. Her published works include more than 120 research papers, 7 monographers and 8 books.

kbaizakova@mail.ru

Prof. Kukeyeva Fatima Turarovna is the heading *Kazakhstan Chair* of the International Relations and Foreign Policy of Kazakhstan, Department of International Relations of Al-Farabi Kazakh National University, Almaty. She is director of the Resource Center for the American and Democratic Studies at the KazNU. Her published works include *China and Russia: The Risk of Uncoordinated US-EU Strategies* (Almaty, 2003); *USA and EU Strategy in Central Asia: Geopolitics and Security* (Moscow, 2003); *Bush Doctrine: Analyses of the US Foreign Policy Strategy* (Almaty, 2004); *US and Russian Strategy in Central Asia* (Taiwan, 2005); *Central Asia in the US Foreign Policy*, (Almaty, 2005) and *Central Asian Security and the International Terrorism Combating Problem*, (Uzbekistan, 2005).

fturar@mail.ru

About the Contributors

Dr. Anita Sengupta is Fellow at the Maulana Abul Kalam Azad Institute of Asian Studies, Kolkata. She has contributed articles on boundaries and state formation, the question of minorities and minority identity, gender, problems of transitional polities and culture in the Central Asian region to several national and international research journals such as the *Central Asian Survey, Journal of Central Asian Studies* and *Central Asia and the Caucasus.* Dr. Sengupta has been an invited speaker at various national and international seminars. She is the author of *Russia, China and Multilateralism in Central Asia,* New Delhi: Shipra Publications, 2005; *The Formation of the Uzbek Nation-State: A Study in Transition,* Lanham, Boulder, New York, Toronto, Oxford: Lexington Books, 2003 and *Frontiers into Borders: The Transformation of Identities in Central Asia,* Delhi and London: Hope India Publications and Greenwich Millennium Press Ltd, 2002.

anitasengupta@hotmail.com

Prof. Baizakova Kuralay Irtysovna is currently Dean of the Department of International Relations, Al-Farabi Kazakh National University, Almaty. She is also director of the European Documentation Centre (Al-Farabi KazNU) since 2002 and the chief editor of *European Dialogue* magazine. She is director of the NATO Resource and Information Centre since 2006 at the KazNU. She was honoured with the best supervisor of students' scientific researches by Ministry of Education and Science of the Republic of Kazakhstan. Prof. Baizakova was awarded with the honour of *The best Lecturer of the year 2005* by the Ministry of Education and Science for her contribution in the fields of European and American history, international relations, theory of international relations, problems of regional and national security, international security structures, regional conflicts and their resolution, process of European integration and security problems in Central Asian region. Her published works include more than 120 research papers, 7 monographers and 8 books.

kbaizakova@mail.ru

Khojamakhmad Umarov is currently the Head of Department at the Institute of Economic Research, Ministry of Economic Development and Trade, Tajikistan. He is specializes in the area of bilateral and multilateral economic and trade cooperation. He has contributed several research papers/chapters to national/international journal and volumes respectively.

umarov2000@mail.ru

Prof. Burnashev Rustam is currently working at the Department of Social Sciences of Kazakh-German University. Earlier, he was co-director of the Research Center for International Relations Analysis, and Head of the project 'Theory and Practice of National and Regional Security'. His areas of expertise include military and political aspects of security in Central Asia, theory of international security, research methods in international relations, contemporary French philosophy, logic, methodology and philosophy of science. His selected publications include *Examining Intelligence Cooperation against Terrorist Targets: Phase II,* Garmisch-Partenkirchen: G. Marshall European Center for Security Studies, 2007), and *Islamist Recruitment Mechanisms in Europe: Phase II,* Garmisch-Partenkirchen: G. Marshall European Center for Security Studies.

burnashev@hotmail.com

Dr. Chernykh Irina Aleksandrovna is associate professor at the Department of International Relations, Al-Farabi Kazakh National University. She is the head of the Chair of Regional Studies and World Economy at the university. Her major areas of research are theory and methodology of international security, military and political issues in Central Asia, theory of international relations, research methods and integration process in Europe. Her published works include *Modernization Processes in Central Asia: Models of the Future* (Almaty, 2004), *Central Asia in European Union Foreign Policy* (Almaty, 2004) and *Conditions for Securitization of International*

Terrorism in Central Asia (Spring, 2005). She is a member of the Educational Expert Committee, Soros Foundation in Kazakhstan, Central Asia Work Group for Peace Consortium, Defense Academies and Security Studies Institutes (since 2001), Kazakhstan Fulbright Association (since 2001) and Kazakhstan Political Science Association (since 1998).

chernykhi@yahoo.com

Dr. Makasheva Klara Naldibekovna is professor at the Chair of Regional Studies and World Economy of Al-Farabi Kazakh National University. Her scientific interests include Kazakhstan foreign policy, history of international relations, process of European integration, international organizations, multilateral diplomacy and political system of western countries. She has published more than 70 research papers.

m.klara@mail.ru

Galiev Anuar Abitaevich is associate professor at the Kazakhstan Institute of Management Economics and Prognoses under the President of the Republic of Kazakhstan. Dr. Abitaevich's selected publications are the *Greenwood Encyclopedia of World Folklore and Folklife / Vol.2* Westport, Connecticut – London Greenwood Press. 2006; *Rethinking and Mythologization of the history of the Turkic Peoples in the CIS,* Muqayisali adabiyyat II Beynaxalq konfrans, Baki, 2006 and *Modern History of Kazakhstan,* Almaty, 2005. Dr. Abitaevich is member of the 'Altaistic Studies' (Russian Academy of Science, Moscow), editorial board 'Cultural Values' (Russia-Italy), and Kazakhstan Antic Society.

Urozbayeva Gulmaidan Amanzholovna is senior lecturer at Department of International Relations, Al-Farabi Kazakh National University. Earlier, she was working at the Department of Oriental Manuscripts, History and Culture at the Institute of Oriental Studies named after R.B. Suleimenov under the Ministry of Education and Science of the Republic of Kazakhstan. Her publications include *Customary Law of Nomad Peoples of Eurasia: Common and Particular (comparative analysis)*; *Velikaya Yasa Chingis-hana i istoricheskaya preemstvennost' kazahskogo obychnogo prava//* materialy mezhdunarodnoi nauchno-prakticheskoi konferencii, posvyashennoi desyatiletiyu nezavisimosti Respubliki Kazahstan / Central'no-Aziatskii Universitet, Universitet im. D.A. Kunaeva.

– 2001 s.186-190, Sravnitel'no-sopostavitel'nyi analiz kazahskogo obychnogo prava s obychnym pravom kalmykov Ih Caaz // Materialy mezhdunarodnoi nauchno-prakticheskoi konferencii, posvyashennoi desyatiletiyu nezavisimosti Respubliki Kazahstan // materialy mezhdunarodnoi nauchno-prakticheskoi konferencii, posvyashennoi desyatiletiyu nezavisimosti Respubliki Kazahstan / Central'no-Aziatskii Universitet, Universitet im. D.A. Kunaeva. – 2001 s.49-52; Yasa of Chingiz Khan in Historical and Literatury Sources // second interdisciplinary conference on comparative literature, November 24-24,2006, Baku, Azerbaijan.

gulmaidanurozbayeva@yahoo.com

Prof. Kukeyeva Fatima Turarovna is the heading *Kazakhstan Chair* of the International Relations and Foreign Policy of Kazakhstan, Department of International Relations of Al-Farabi Kazakh National University, Almaty. She is director of the Resource Center for the American and Democratic Studies at the KazNU. Her published works include *China and Russia: The Risk of Uncoordinated US-EU Strategies* (Almaty, 2003); *USA and EU Strategy in Central Asia: Geopolitics and Security* (Moscow, 2003); *Bush Doctrine: Analyses of the US Foreign Policy Strategy* (Almaty, 2004); *US and Russian Strategy in Central Asia* (Taiwan, 2005); *Central Asia in the US Foreign Policy,* (Almaty, 2005) and *Central Asian Security and the International Terrorism Combating Problem,* (Uzbekistan, 2005).

fturar@mail.ru

Prof. Gubaidullina Mara Shaukatovna is teaching at the Department of International Relations and Foreign Policy of the Republic of Kazakhstan, Al-Farabi Kazakh National University. She is a member of editorial board of the *KazGU Herald, International Relations and International Law* and *European Dialog*. She has authored more than 200 research papers on the problems of international relations, stability and security in Central Asia, Caspian region, political and economical problems in European Union, and Germany. She is heading a project on *Democracy in Germany and Europe*.

maragu@mail.ru

Sapanov Seifulla Zhumabaevich is at the Department of International Relations, Al-Farabi KazNU. His areas of research are problem of political systems transformation in Central Asia, international relations and geopolitics in Central Asia. He is a member of editors of the magazine of Kazakhstan Institute of Strategic Studies (KazISS) under the President of the Republic of Kazakhstan. He has more than 75 research publications related to international relations and foreign policy.

cefosh@mail.ru

Prof. P.L. Dash is currently Director of the Centre of Central Eurasian Studies. Over the last about more than two decades besides publishing books, he has contributed to several edited volumes and academic journals over 100 articles and research papers on various issues concerning the former USSR, Russia and Central Asian States and India's relations with these countries.

pldash@hotmail.com

Akatayeva Aliya Askarovna is a senior lecturer at the Department of International Relations, Al-Farabi Kazakh National University. She completed PhD in history of international relations and foreign policy. Her areas of research are Kazakh-India relations; Kazakh-Chinese relations, foreign policy of Kazakhstan and Shanghai Cooperation Organization. She has published *Kazakhstan-China: Trade and Economic Relations*// Himalayan and Central Asian studies (Journal of Himalayan research and cultural foundation, New-Delhi)/ vol.10 N4, October-December 2006; *Security Issues in Central Asia and the Shanghai Cooperation Organization* and *SCO and India's Interests*// KazNU Vestnik, No. 3 (19), 2008;

akatayeva@mail.ru

Karatayeva Lessya Rollanovna is associate professor at the Department of International Relations and Foreign Policy, Al-Farabi Kazakh National University. Her publications include *Concept of Terrorism on the Legislation of Central Asian States*// Kazakhstan-Spectrum No. 1, 2008, pp. 40-46; *Threat of the International Terrorism and its Perception in Kazakhstan; Modern Terrorism: Factors and Tendencies of its Distribution,* (materials of republican scientifically-practical conference. Astana, 2008), *Problemes des effopts collectifs de lutte contre le terrorisme international en Asie Centrale* (L'Asie Centrale et La Securite Regionale Les Cahiers du GREDFIC, Numero 2, 2007). Her research interests include theory and methodology of analysis of regional conflicts,

problems of construction of system antiterrorist activity in Central Asia and theoretical and methodological analysis of security issues.
lessya.karataeva@gmail.com

Prof. Kuldip Singh is director, Centre for Central and South Asian Studies, Guru Nanak Dev University, Amritsar, India.
kuldipsingh2004@yahoo.co.in

Prof. R.G. Gidadhubli, former director of the Centre of Central Eurasian Studies, University of Mumbai, is an economist specializing on Russian and Central Asian economies and on the economic transition of the commonwealth of Independent States. Over the last about four decades besides publishing 5 books, he has contributed to several edited volumes and academic journals over 300 articles and research papers on various economic issues concerning the former USSR, Russia and Central Asian States and India's economic relations with these countries.
rgidadhubli@hotmail.com

Dr. Jyotsna Bakshi is currently working at the India Chair, University of World Economy and Diplomacy, Tashkent. From 2002-2005, she worked at the India Chair at the Osh State University. She has also worked as a Research Fellow in the Institute for Defence Studies and Analyses, New Delhi. Earlier, she has done research work in the Institute of Oriental Studies, Moscow (Academy of Sciences) and has extensively travelled in Russia and Central Asia. She has published more than 65 research papers and articles and three books: 1. *Russia and India from Ideology to Geopolitics*, Delhi 1999; 2. *Russia-China Relations: Relevance for India*, Delhi 2004. 3. (Ed.) *India's engagement with Central Asia with focus on India-Uzbekistan Relations*, Tashkent 2007.
jyotsnabakshi2002@yahoo.com

Dr. Nivedita Das Kundu is Research Fellow at the Indian Council of World Affairs (ICWA), New Delhi. Earlier, she was Associate Fellow with the Institute of Defence Studies and Analyses (IDSA), New Delhi. She has recently authored a book on *Russia and its Near Abroad: Strategic Dynamics and Implications*. She has contributed extensively on her area of research nationally and internationally.
dr.niveditadaskundu@gmail.com

1

Reclaiming Eurasia: Eurasianism and Contemporary Kazakh Politics

Anita Sengupta

INTRODUCTION

Encyclopaedic definitions of Eurasia note that Eurasia is the landmass composed of the continents of Europe and Asia. It can be considered a supercontinent, part of a supercontinent of Africa-Eurasia or simply a continent.

In plate tectonics, the Eurasian plate includes Europe and most of Asia but not the Indian sub-continent and the area east of the Cherskiy Range in East Siberia. Eurasia is also used in international politics as a neutral way to refer to organizations or affairs concerning the post-Soviet states. Europeans traditionally consider Europe and Asia to be separate continents with the dividing line placed along the Dardanelles, Bosphorous, Caucasus mountains, Ural river and Ural mountains; and, this terminology spread to the rest of the world. History proves this to be a geopolitical division. In reality the two continents are actually one. Anthropologically, historically and linguistically Eurasia is more appropriately, though vaguely, subdivided into West Eurasia (often including North Africa) and East Eurasia and it is further subdivided into regions like Europe, East Asia, South Asia, Central Asia and South-West Asia which have distinct cultural, religious, historic and linguistic features. Alternatively, some historians perceive much of South Europe, South Asia and West Asia as historically closer to each other than to their northern counterparts; thus creating a vague South Eurasia. North Europe and parts of North Asia create another vaguely similar cultural and geographical sphere known as North Eurasia.[1]

Eurasia as a distinct geocultural space – not entirely separated from Europe but functioning as a contradistinction of the conventional paradigms of 'east' and 'west' – remains significant even today. There remains a discomfort with both European and Asian archetypes though an attempt at cultural bridging that undermines conventional dichotomies and engages the identity of the steppe is on. The idea of Eurasia has also opened up new possibilities of imagining geographical space. Aleksandr Dugin for instance points to a particular way of imagining the space when he notes, "Eurasia does not have fixed boundaries. Eurasia is a civilizational structure, it is a geopolitical pole".[2] The term Eurasia or *Evraziia* was used by Eurasianists to indicate a different 'geographical world', different from both Europe and Asia. It has been argued that the Eurasianists' 'geographical world' of Eurasia can be called a mega-region.[3] Eurasianist sometimes used the word 'continent' to refer to this mega-region but that usage was for them metaphorical rather than scientific. This conception however, problematized the word 'continent'. In this new world of Russia-Eurasia, Eurasianists declared cultural independence from both Europe and Asia. Eurasianists strongly identified ethnic Russians with other Eastern Slavs and people of the Eurasian mega-region, Finno-Ugric, Turkic and Mongolian. Eurasianists did not however define the boundaries of Eurasia with precision and various versions of Eurasia overlapped. Yet, the expanse of their Eurasias roughly coincided with the boundaries of pre-1914 Russian Empire. To Eurasianists, Eurasia was separated from Asia to its South by high mountains and impenetrable deserts and to its West Eurasia by what Savitskii called the 'region between the Black and the Baltic Seas'. The Eurasianists devised a series of detailed arguments to justify this as the legitimate geographical divide. A strict interpretation of this geographical scheme excluded all of Russia's territory east of the Lena River. On the other hand some regions that fall outside Russia's political borders – a large part of western China for instance – was seen as an integral part of Eurasia. Eurasianists argued that there is no discernable break across the Urals, linguistically, culturally and economically.

The Eurasianist current developed in the 1920s inside Russian intellectuals who had immigrated to Western Europe after the October Revolution, including Petr N. Savitskii, George Vernadskii and Nikolai S. Trubetskoi. Nikolai Sergeevich Trubetskoi, an ethnographer and philologist, claimed that the Eurasian continent had served as the arena for the formation and development of a distinct civilization and culture, a civilization that absorbed and blended both European and Asiatic elements, that belonged to neither realm. His vision of the territorial contours of this continent coincided, in large measure, with those of the Russian Empire with the exception of its western borderlands in Finland, the Baltic regions and Poland. Across these broad spaces, Eurasia was a zone of profound ethnographic diversity made up of a core of Russians, Ugro-Finnic peoples and the Turkic populations of the Volga Basin, Siberia and Central Asia. Russia's geographical existence within a larger zone of Eurasian civilization meant that Russian culture had been shaped to a not insignificant extent by influences coming from Asia, a conclusion which Trubetskoi used to underscore and enhance Russia's elemental differentiation from Europe. Referring to a wide historical array of manifestations of Russian culture, he emphasized the pre-eminent importance of connections to the east as compared to those of the west. He argued that the Russians, Ugro-Finns and Volga Turks comprise a cultural zone that has connections with both the Slavs and the Turanian East and that it was difficult to identify which was more important. He went on to note that Russia was Eurasian and not European (Slavic), not only by virtue of its cultural patterns but in terms of anthropological-racial considerations as well. He observed,

> Turkic blood mingles in Russian veins with that of Ugro-Finns and the Slavs. It is usually forgotten that our brothers (if not in language or faith, then in blood, character and culture) are not only the Slavs but the Turanians.[4]

Mark Bassin argues that Trubetskoi's ideas on the implications of Eurasia's geographic character were ultimately intended to prepare a new conceptual ground in support the need to maintain the unity and integrity of the historic spaces of the Russian state.[5] Bassin goes on to argue that Trubetskoi's position of Russia-Eurasia has to be understood in the context of post-War European and trans-Atlantic discourse of self-determination. He explicitly associated Russia with the colonial realms of the non-European world with a view to appropriating for post revolutionary Russia the same principles and standards that were now being accorded to other post-colonial regions. Bassin argues that Trubetskoi replaced imperial Russia with the alternative of Eurasia as the legitimate repository of the national sovereignty of all groups across the continental expanse. He noted that, by virtue of the pluralism of ethnic groups, Eurasia was a "peculiar" type of nation and the development of a pan-Eurasian nationalism was necessary to provide a sense of unity necessary for a viable state. This "peculiar multi-ethnic state" possessing its own nationalism would be Eurasian, its territory Eurasia and its nationalism Eurasianism.[6] While Trubetskoi interpreted Russian history in such a way as to recognize Turkic Muslims as an integral element of Russian identity, Tatar reformers like Ismail Bey Gaspirali conceptualized Turkic Muslim identity to include co-existence with the Russian people as one of its fundamental tenants. This has been interpreted as a counterpart to the pan-Eurasianist ideas expressed by Trubetskoi a century later.[7]

There is, today, a need to take note that the Eurasian debate itself is not a monolithic whole and in its various forms serves distinct purposes. Caroline Humphrey has noted that the concept of 'Eurasia' has enabled the governing circles of many Asian regions of Russia to create distinctive ideas about the nature of their existence within the Federation. What seems to be emerging are multiple visions where each region has its own perspectives. However, the idea of 'Eurasia' is also providing an arena for new political relations to be formed between the provinces. She has argued that Eurasia is likely to be highly influential both in conceptualizing federal relations and in shaping the political-cultural character of the constituent regions.[8] However, not all reactions to Eurasianism have been positive. There have been critiques like Urkhanova from Buryatia who have argued that Eurasianism is built on Russian great power statehood. As a result the 'imprecise inclusiveness' of Eurasianism is a cloak for renewed Russian imperialism. Yet, she argues that the Buryats cannot refuse Eurasia as they have been part of it during the Soviet period.[9] However Humphrey notes that the idea of Eurasia has resurfaced among the new generation of leaders in the Inner Asian regions and Central Asia as an escape from their peripherality. She argues that it provides an arena of political imagination where the Inner Asian people can claim a dignified place. This has meant that there now exist various regional Eurasian perspectives. It has, therefore, been argued that Eurasia is more than simply Russian Eurasianism and it is important to take into account non-Russians who have sought to imagine this vast space. This article examines how the Eurasian idea, that had taken shape at the turn of the last century, has now been creatively appropriated by contemporary Kazakh politics.

KAZAKHSTAN AND EURASIA

Over the years, Eurasia has become a flexible concept used by different Kazakh political and intellectual actors for different agendas. For instance, the Eurasian dimension of Russian and Central Asian geography and history has been claimed by a contemporary Kazakh poet, polemist, environmentalist, politician and diplomat, Olzhas Suleimanov in his book *AZiIA*. It has been argued that Suleimanov in his book has questioned the boundaries of "Russia" Eurasia as a shared space and has attempted to come to an understanding of how to reconcile its destiny as a unified state with the local and contradictory aspirations of its constitutive ethnic groups. However, while arguing in favour of the ethnic dignity of his people, Suleimanov's ultimate vision has been one of synthesis and inter-dependence between the Slav and the Turk. He believes that this ideal of cultural reciprocity flourished in Eurasia's remote past and it is the recovering of this past that is the task of the creative writer. In *AZiIA,* he attempts this by searching for Turkic lexical and narrative elements in one of medieval Russia's celebrated literary artefacts, *The Song of Igor's Campaign*.[10]

Suleimanov had attempted a creative interpretation of the Eurasian space. In the present context, Eurasianism assumes significance only to the extent that it becomes a part of the real world debate and influences Kazakh policies. In fact, within Kazakhstan Suleimanov's position has been echoed both by political analysts and the political leadership in recent times. For instance D. Nazarbaeva writes:

> Kazakhstan ... is a Eurasian state strongly influenced by Europe and Western values. Contrary to what certain politicians and journalists assert we are not another *stan*. Saudi Arabia is not our historical landmark; we look to Norway, South Korea and Singapore.[11]

The Eurasian idea became a doctrine in November 2003 when the International Institute of Contemporary Politics (Kazakhstan) published a report entitled *Kazakhstan, Rossia, Ukraina: Liderskaia Troika Evrazii* (Kazakhstan, Russia, Ukraine: Three Leaders of Eurasia).[12] This alliance was justified on the grounds that, in the course of the previous years, the three countries had acquired a new infrastructure of state institutions, created institutions of market economy and generated stable political conditions. Similarly the three are faced with the tasks of creating an efficient state system which is moving away from raw materials to high tech economic sectors, better conditions of personnel rotation, stemming illegal migration, integrating with the global economy under conditions conducive to higher living, stronger human rights and creation of a civil society. The idea that Kazakhstan and the other Central Asian states (surrounded by Russia, China and South Asia), constitute the geopolitical centerpiece of the Eurasian continent has been underlined in contemporary Kazakh strategic writings. From the purely strategic and geopolitical perspective, analysts like Murat Laumulin have argued in favour of the emerging significance of Eurasia. Laumulin argues that with the expansion of the EU and NATO, opportunities will be created for connecting West European and Eurasian security. He notes that in future instead of the notion of 'Atlantic Europe' the idea of a dominant 'Eurasian Europe' will emerge.[13]

Among the Soviet successor states, Kazakh President Nazarbaev has been the most consistent promoter of the idea of Eurasianism. While President Nazarbaev's ideas have an indirect link to those of the *evraziitsy* of the 1920s, this remains a rhetorical link and the President selectively adopts these ideas stemming based on his reading of the country's geopolitical and demographic circumstances. Among other considerations is the fact that at the time of independence Kazakhstan's economic infrastructure was arguably more integrated with Russia's than that of any other newly independent state. However, it has been argued that official Kazakh Eurasianism should not be interpreted exclusively as a foreign policy strategy and a doctrine of economic realism favourable to the preservation of privileged relations with the former Soviet republics and especially with Russia. Kazakh Eurasianism has a domestic aspect relating to the country's ethnic balance which has encouraged the President to emphasize the 'mixed culture' of the Kazakhs and their affinity not to the South but to the North.[14] Vinkovetsky argues that President Nazarbaev also conceived of Eurasianist ideas as a means for overcoming ethnic divisions and as a multi-ethnic replacement for the untenable Soviet identity. President Nazarbaev's Eurasia rhetoric – the idea that all ethnic groups who live in Kazakhstan today have a rightful place in the heart of Eurasia – serves as an instrument of nation building.[15]

Kazakhstan also shares a long land border with Russia. This has meant that, even as the policies of Nazarbaev's government have shifted his rhetorical commitment to Eurasia has remained unchanged. He regularly makes Eurasianist speeches at the Lev Gumiliev Eurasianist University in Astana which is held as an example of the institutionalization of Eurasianism as an official ideology. The website of the university cites clearly that it was established by a decree of the President in May 1996 "taking into consideration the expanding international contacts of the Republic of Kazakhstan, its active participation in world integration processes and implementation of the idea of Eurasian Union". It goes on to note that the university is a concrete realization of the idea of Eurasianism.[16] The President has also created an Eurasianist Centre at the university with the mission of formulating a distinctively Kazakh Eurasian ideology different from its Russian counterpart.

At the practical level, Kazakh efforts at integration on the Eurasian level have involved numerous initiatives. Kazakhstan has emerged as a leader in efforts at promotion of regional economic and political integration in Eurasia. Under President Nazarbaev, Kazakhstan has followed a foreign policy that has sought to maintain good relations with the most important external powers. In addition there has been an attempt to strengthen ties with countries of Central Asia and the Caspian Sea basin. Kazakhstan also plays a prominent role in most of Eurasia's international institutions and organizations like the Commonwealth of Independent States, the Collective Security Treaty Organization, the Eurasian Economic Community, the Shanghai Cooperation Organization, the North Atlantic Treaty Organization and the Organization for Security and Cooperation in Europe. The President wishes to make Kazakhstan a 'transcontinental economic bridge':

> Occupying the position midway between Europe and Asia and serving as a lively arena for economic and political contacts, Kazakhstan is now able to act as a link in the chain connecting the two great civilizations of East and West.[17]

In keeping goal, there have been efforts at improving regional transportation, pipelines and communication networks, reducing customs and other barriers to trade, encouraging tourism, strengthening labour mobility in Eurasia and promoting Kazakh private investment in other Eurasian economies. The strong Kazakh support for regional integration results in part from a recognition that Kazakhstan will benefit from enhanced ties among Eurasian countries. There is also a conviction that through this integration at the Eurasian level Kazakhstan and its neighbours will achieve greater room to manoeuvre among great powers active in the region and reduce the risk of their becoming dependent on any one supplier, customer or market. An increase in regional prosperity would ensue from this integration. It has been argued that Kazakhstan's geography allowed it to exercise decisive influence in two of Eurasia's most important sub-regions – Central Asia and the Caspian Sea.[18]

Kazakhstan has repeatedly presented proposals for a Eurasian Union covering a range of cooperative endeavours in politics, economics and security. The idea of a Eurasian Union was conceived in the mid 1990s and was intended to promote economic, social and to a limited degree political integration across the post-Soviet space. It was focused initially establishing a Customs Union, a common economic space and to enable citizens of the post-Soviet successor states to travel visa-free across the new borders. President Nazarbaev argued that the Commonwealth of Independent States has been impotent. In contrast, the Eurasian Union would be empowered by an executive Committee and a Parliament. President Nazarbaev argued that much of the world is integrating; and, in the post-Soviet space, this integration should work better since it was an integrated economic space. This initiative failed. President Nazarbaev launched a new initiative in April 2007 that focused on border and water management issues that had long complicated relations among the Central Asian states. The November 2007 decision to give Kazakhstan chairmanship of the Organization for Security and Cooperation in Europe (OSCE) in 2010 recognizes the country's growing importance in Eurasia.

Kazakh officials have characterized this as an endorsement of the country's successful economic and political reforms, its leading role in Central Asia and its role as a bridge between the former Soviet republics and other OSCE members.

On the broader international front the rhetorical significance of the Eurasian Union, the President said:

> It is absolutely clear to us that the main tendency in the world today is global integration and the inspiring example of the Member Countries of the European Union which is finding support in the various regions of the world. Moves towards unification are evident in Latin America, South-East Asia and the Near East. Along the same lines is the idea advanced by Kazakhstan for the creation of a Eurasian Union on the territory of the former Soviet Union. This not only advances obvious economic objectives but also pursues integration of the former Soviet Republics in the fields of science, culture, education and information. I am sure that in the next century and beyond, the united sub-continent of Europe and Asia would develop as a single unit for the benefit of our children and our descendants. There will come a day when Europe and Asia will develop together, drawing upon their huge natural and human resources.[19]

President Nazarbaev has also called for the establishment of a Eurasian Research Centre that will focus on the unique spiritual heritage of the Eurasian people.

President Nazarbaev's idea of a 'Eurasian' space, therefore, serves several aims. It has been argued that one of the most important is that it situates his country squarely in the centre of a far greater and potentially more consequential entity.[20] At first sight Kazakhstan is a landlocked state far from the world's principal land routes, faces with a precarious trade balance and a difficult geopolitical situation. President Nazarbaev says:

> From the vantage point at the centre of Eurasia we can easily see that there is a process of building new systems of international security going on in the West. For example, NATO is actively moving eastward directly to the borders of Russia. In the East and the South-East Asian countries are continuing to seek ways of political and military cooperation within the bounds of their structures. If we look at a geographical map, it is easy to notice that there is a consecutive vertical row of countries of Eurasia from Russia in the north to India in the south (Central Asian

> countries, Iran, Pakistan) that does not yet link either with the East or the West. I would call this continuous belt of countries situated along the meridian of the centre of Eurasia the 'belt of anticipation'.
>
> Despite all the differences among these countries, they constitute a relatively solid group from the point of view of resources and possibilities of influencing not only the balance of power in Asia or Eurasia but even the geopolitical balance of the world. Security in Europe, and especially in Asia relations between global economic centres of Western Europe and Southeastern Asia, will to a significant degree depend on how the countries of this geopolitical 'belt of anticipation' decide their positions and orientation.
>
> The biggest and so far the mightiest of these countries is Russia. Precisely her choice will decide stability in the world and in Eurasia.[21]

Nazarbaev further argues that, since Russia will never be admitted as an equal member into either the European or the East Asian sphere, its only viable choice is to unite countries in the 'belt of anticipation' into a new security system. He then argues that Kazakhstan would be an essential partner to Russia in this regard, given her strategic and central position in such a geopolitical construct.

Nazarbaev's 'belt of anticipation' is interesting because it indicates a vertical definition of the Eurasian space that is generally visualized as a horizontal expanse. It is also significant in terms of the actual states that are included: Russia, India, Central Asian republics, Iran and Pakistan. The definition excludes Afghanistan. What is also significant is that this definition places Kazakhstan squarely in the centre of this imagined Eurasia. In fact, it has been argued that President Nazarbaev has moved his capital so that it coincides with the centre of Eurasia as he defines it. But then there is another dimension to Nazarbaev's Eurasia. It is also conceived of as a Union intended to promote a common economic space across the territory of the former Soviet Union. Nazarbaev was clear in pointing out that this was not meant as a restoration of the Soviet Union but as a post-Soviet construct that loosely resembles the European Union.

In a sense, this vertical definition has precedence in the vision of a North-South linkage as an alternative transport route that would link Russia, Iran and India. The corridor was conceived as stretching from ports in India to the southern Iranian port of Bandar

Abbas where goods would transit Iran and the Caspian Sea ports in the Russian sector of the Caspian. From there the route would stretch along the Volga River via Moscow to northern Europe. Along with Russia, India and Iran, this project was subsequently joined by Belarus, Kazakhstan, Tajikistan and Azerbaijan. More recently, Turkmen President Berdymukhammedov in his meetings with Iranian leaders has expressed interest in the project.[22]

A series of alternative 'Eurasias' have emerged over time. Contemporary Kazakh definitions provide a number of alternatives that this article has explored.

In the present context, Eurasianism assumes significance to the extent that it posits alternative paths of development that challenges the rhetoric of nationalist politics. Its institutionalization is still in the making through political and economic initiatives across its vast space. This institutionalization has led to the Collective Security Treaty being now renamed the Collective Security Treaty Organization and the Shanghai Five has become the Shanghai Cooperation Organization. The effectiveness of such institutionalization will depend on both on developments in the international arena as well as developments within the Eurasian space. It is in this context that 'reclaiming Eurasia' assumes significance for an understanding of contemporary Kazakh politics.

NOTES AND REFERENCES

1. In ethnographic terms Eurasia has been divided into1. Sino-Mongol-Turkic area 2. Indo-European orb 3. the Semitic region see Come Carpentier De Gourdon, "The Eurasian Saga: Presence of the Past", *World Affairs,* Vol 8, No 1, January-March 2004.
2. Aleksandr Dugin, *Geopoltika Postmoderna Vremena Noviekh Imperrii Ocherki Geopolitiki XXI Veka,* St Petersburg: Amfora, 2007.
3. Ilya'Vinkovetsky, "Eurasia and its Uses: the History of An Idea and the Mental Geography of Post Soviet Space', unpublished paper presented at the 2007 Annual Soyuz Symposium on *Locating Eurasia in Postsocialist Studies: The Geopolitics of Naming, April 27-29, 2007, Princeton University.*
4. N.S. Trubetzkoy, "The Upper and Lower Stories of Russian Culture", in *The Legacy of Ghengis Khan and Other Essays,* Ann Arbor: Michigan Slavic Publication, 1991, cited from Mark Bassin, "Classical Eurasianism and the Geopolitics of Russian Identity",http://www.dartmouth.edu/~crn/crn_papers/Basin.pdf

5. Bassin, "Classical Eurasianism and the Geopolitics of Russian Identity".
6. N.S. Trubetzkoy, "Pan-Eurasian Nationalism" cited from Bassin, "Classical Eurasianism and the Geopolitics of Russian Identity".
7. See Sener Akturk, "Identity Crisis: Russia's Muslims in the debate over Russian identity vis a vis Europe" *UC Davis International Affairs Journal* Vol 2 No 1, Fall 2005.
8. Caroline Humphrey, "Eurasia, ideology and the political imagination in provincial Russia", in C. M. Hann (ed) *Postsocialism Ideas, ideologies and practices in Eurasia,* London and New York: Routledge, 1993.
9. See Humphrey, "Eurasia, ideology and the political imagination in provincial Russia".
10. For details see Harsha Ram, "Imagining Eurasia: The Poetics and Ideology of Olzhas Seleimanov's *AZ i IA*", *Slavic Review,* Vol 60 No 2, Summer 2001.
11. D. Nazarbaeva, "Spetsifika I perspektivy politicheskogo razvitia Kazakhstana", *Bulletin* No 3, 2003 http://iimp.kz/index.php?action=show&art_id=150&from=5.
12. See http://iimp.kz/index.php?action=show&art_id=150&from=5.
13. Murat T. Laumulin *The Geopolitics of XXI Century Central Asia,* KISI: Almaty 2007.
14. See Marlene Laruelle, *Russia's Central Asian Policy and the Role of Russian Nationalism,,* Silk Road Paper April 2008, http://www.isdp.eu/files/publications/srp/08/m108russiacentral.pdf
15. Vinkovetsky, "Eurasia and its Uses: the History of An Idea and the Mental Geography of Post Soviet Space'.
16. See the L.N. Gumilyov Eurasian National University website at www.emu.kz.
17. *Address by H. E. Mr Nursultan Nazarbaev, President of the Republic of Kazakhstan to the twenty-eighth session of the General Conference of the United Nations Educational, Scientific and Cultural Organization,* Paris, November 15, 1995.
18. Richard Weitz, *Kazakhstan and the New International Politics of Eurasia,* Silk Road Paper, July 2008, Central Asia-Caucasus Institurte and Silk Road Studies Programme, www.silkroadstudies.org.
19. From the *Address by H.E. Nursultan Nazarbaev, President of the Republic of Kazakhstan to the Twenty-Eighth Session of the General Conference of the United Nations Educational, Scientific and Cultural Organization.*
20. Vinkovetsky, "Eurasia and its Uses: the History of An Idea and the Mental Geography of Post Soviet Space'.
21. N.A. Nazarbaev, "Sniat's Evrazii 'polias vyzhidaniia' , Interview in *Kazakhstanskaia Pravda,* Almaty October 21, 1995 cited from Vinkovetsky, "Eurasia and its Uses: the History of An Idea and the Mental Geography of Post Soviet Space'.
22. "Central Asia: Turkmenistan Pushing North-South Trade Corridor with Iran", *Radio Free Europe/Radio Liberty,* Wednesday, June 20, 2007.

2

Evolution of Presidentship in the Republic of Kazakhstan

K.N. Baizakova

INTRODUCTION

A significant events of the 20th century was the break-up of the Soviet political system. But the transition to democracy had demonstrated systemic change and also continuity of this very process. Now it has become obvious that this process is not a sort of continuity. Rather, it was a combination of several phases with its own peculiarities.

After declaring its independence on 16 December 1991, Kazakhstan entered the first phase of transition in which fundamental changes in the former political and economic processes were expected. This was the phase of creation of a new political system. The first and then the second Constitution were adopted; Presidential and parliamentary elections were held; and democratic political institutions started to function. Kazakh society was experiencing unique changes that were connected with several difficult "transitions". Objective analysis of unprecedented social reforms in the post-Soviet states, including Kazakhstan, shows that the transition to democracy is not a linear process and may be fraught with serious threats to the socio-political development of the country.

A characteristic feature of the constitutional development of independent Kazakhstan is that the reform of the whole political system being carried out by the state itself. It is noteworthy that Kazakhstan was able to avoid political crises which might have led to destabilization of society. Clean and positive results have been achieved in Kazakhstan's evolutionary reformation of the political system with a Presidential system of rule.

The institution of President in Kazakhstan has form in an environment with a combination of political and economic systems.[1] Since then it has undergone evolution in many respects. The institution of President was introduced in the Constitution of 1993. It is true that the provisions of the first Constitution of independent Kazakhstan were so restrictive that it hardly a Presidential form of rule in the classical sense.

On 30 August 1995, a national referendum was conducted which approved the new Constitution. On 5 September, the day the results of the referendum were published, the Constitution came into force.[2] Kazakh scholars have rightly pointed out that as per the new Constitution the main feature of the system of rule in Kazakhstan is a strong Presidential system.[3]

The President of Kazakhstan, N.A. Nazarbaev has said:

> The Constitution of Kazakhstan, through it statutes, has laid the foundation of a strong Presidential Republic and division of authority between various branches of power. Institutions of civil society have been formed, human rights are being observed, mass media is working in a free atmosphere. The revived statehood of Kazakhstan forms the basis for building up democracy and a market economy.[4]

In Kazakhstan, as in other post-Soviet countries, building up of a national sovereign state is taking place simultaneously with their inclusion in the globalization process. Radical transformation of social and economic systems was initiated even though there was lack of experience and absence of democratic traditions in society.

Looking at the developments taking place in today's world, we must admit that globalization has become an objective reality which is connected with the functioning of a world market economy as a system by itself. Globalization is influencing not only the existing world order; it is also directly influencing the internal political scene and the role of the state in this entire process.

Any State should be capable of suitably reacting to new challenges and threats. Under conditions of globalization, the State has to expand its role in socio-economic, political and other areas. It is only the State that can formulate and implement a long-term strategy for the development of the country and make it capable of facing challenges of the twenty-first century.

HOW TO BUILT A STRONG STATE

What are the conditions necessary for the transitional countries for building up a "strong state" of such a kind? How are they to be created?

The process of building up a strong State should start with strengthening of political institutions with Head of State as its centre with the wide powers. The Presidential system of rule by itself has several variations and flexibilities in well-tested democracies of the world. The Kazakh model of Presidential system of rule has acquired its present shape on the basis of the Constitution of 1995.

Presently, the President of Kazakhstan by his position does not have executive functions. His main prerogative is to decide the strategic directions of internal and foreign policies of the country. The Head of State has the right to interfere in the work of representative organ on matters of special importance by taking over legislative functions. That is, the constitutional set up of the Republic of Kazakhstan is such that the President is equidistant from the executive as well the legislature. In this sense, the Presidential system of Kazakhstan is an institution for ensuring harmonious functioning of all the branches of power and ensuring their responsibility to the people. The President of Kazakhstan is an arbiter who maintains balance between various organs of power.[5] While implementing the Presidential system of rule, certain adjustments have been made in division of power, keeping local conditions in mind.

Establishment of the Presidential system of rule in Kazakhstan has been borrowed as a foreign political and state institution. This system is functional in more than 63 countries of the world.

In general, Presidential system in Kazakhstan has been successful during the period of important reforms, proved its worth and established stability. "During the period of transition, a strong Presidential system was in a position to control contradictions that might have posed a threat to national harmony and political stability in Kazakhstan."[6]

Experience shows that a strong Presidential system is not an obstacle in the path of democracy. On the other hand, in France, as well in US, long democratic traditions do not permit anyone, including the President, to trample democracy.

During times of deep crises and unrest, there arises an inevitable need of a regulatory mechanism to pull the country out and bring about socio-economic and socio-political stability. This is particularly seen during periods of fundamental change, downfall of authoritarian regimes and setting of a new political order.

That is why many countries of the world are showing interest in the Presidential system. This political institution means that it is the President who ensures the integrity of the country, optimum and balanced functioning of the legislative, executive and judicial organs as well as being the arbiter in disputes. The greatest advantage of the Presidential system is that it facilitates a unified and stable executive power.

Kazakhstan has used the 1958 model of the French Constitution. A comparative study of the constitutions of Kazakhstan and France shows that Kazakhstan can be called a mixed semi-Presidential Republic.

In France, the authors of the Constitution of 1958 initially wanted to give more powers to the President. But, later, they included in the Constitution several provisions which restricted the powers of the President. In this connection, French scholars have introduced a new concept of "Presidentialization" to explain the specific character of the state system in France. By "Presidentialization" they mean more powers to the President while, simultaneously, strengthening democratic institutions of the society.

The other feature of "Presidentialization" is protection of the post of President from individual temperament, political beliefs and other intentions of the person occupying this post. An example of the independence of President's post was the situation when President F. Mitterrand had a confrontation with Parliament in which the Opposition was in majority. Such a situation did not lead to any constitutional or political crisis as expected by politicians. It rather set an unprecedented example of productive cooperation – "co-existence" – in which every side continued to perform its functions going by 'words' of the Constitution.

The 1995 Constitution of the Republic of Kazakhstan, based on the French model, has given a different kind of status to the President of Kazakhstan. He is Head of State, holds the highest post, is a symbol and guarantor as well as protector of the unity of peoples, of the Constitution, human rights and freedoms.[7] This high status of the President flows from the constitutional character of the country which has accepted the Presidential form of rule.

The doctrine and practice of the Kazakh model of Presidential system is based on the following principles of state power: political and lawful recognition of the universal norm of division of power; adapting the constitutional experience of other countries according to the conditions of Kazakh society; maintenance of political stability by means of legislative regulation of relations between different organs of state power; and an independent legal authority.

Though the institution of President in Kazakhstan has a lot of potential for further growth, there is it still a need to rectify some of the provisions. In order to avoid a situation that may lead to misuse Presidential powers, candidature for the post of future President should be left to political parties. Secondly, it is necessary to develop stable democratic traditions among the citizens. The 1995 Constitution of Kazakhstan helped the country to make the transition to a real sovereign state, a modern, democratic economic order. It has become clear that this process is not a sort of continuity but a combination of different transition phases. Amendments and additions to the Constitution were initiated by the President himself. In May 2007, the Parliament of Kazakhstan passed these amendments and additions.[8]

A special feature of the amendments was that they were oriented towards the growth of Kazakhstan into an economically and democratically strong country. Implementation of these amendments in the Constitution will give further impetus to the economic progress achievements of Kazakhstan along with political stability.

The constitutional reforms have four directions:

- giving more powers to the Parliament;
- more increased role of political parties in the life of the country;
- improving the judicial system and strengthening protection of human rights; and,
- strengthening of local self-government and *Maslihat*s in performing their functions.

The continuing process of democratic reforms calls for increased effectiveness in governance in the sense that organs of state should be able to respond adequately to the changes taking place within the country as well as outside its borders. Ensuring political stability essentially implies building up of a democratic political system which is legitimate and effective in governance.[9]

No less complex is the problem of comprehending socio-political processes to minimize risks to internal political stability and sustainable development of the Kazakh society and state. "Internal security would be long-lasting if it is consolidated by democratic changes in the political system."[10]

By its form of rule Kazakhstan remains a Presidential republic. However, looking at the elements of this form of rule as practiced and tested in the constitutions of various developed democracies, we can say that the Kazakh model of Presidential system is a logical culmination of a specific system of a unified state power in society.

NOTES AND REFERENCES

1. Zakon Kazakhskoi SSR "Ob uchrezhdenii posta Prezidenta Kazakhskoi SSR i vnesenii izmenenii i dopolnenii v Konstitutsiyu Kazakhskoi SSR".
2. Konstitutsiya Respubliki Kazakhstan 1995 goda. – Almaty, 1995.
3. See Nurpeisov E.K., Kotov A.K. Gosudarstvo Kazakhstan: ot khanskoi vlasti–k prezidentskoi respublike. – Almaty, 1995. – p. 67.
4. Nazarbaev N.A. Na poroge XXI veka. – Almaty: Oner – 1998. – p. 165.
5. Konstitutsiya Respubliki Kazakhstan 1995 goda. – Almaty, 1995.
6. Akimbekov S., Syroezhkin K. Respublika Kazakhstan: poisk putei ustoichivovo razvitiya / / Tsentralnaya Aziya i Kavkaz. – 1999. – No. 2.- p. 121.
7. Konstitutsiya Respubliki Kazakhstan 1995 goda. – Almaty, 1995. – Article 48.
8. Zakon Respubliki Kazakhstan. O vnesenii izmenenii i dopolnenii v Konstitutsiyu Respubliki Kazakhstan/ /Kazakhstanskaya Pravda. – 22 May 2007.
9. Bizhanov A.Kh. Stabilnost v Kazakhstane: sostoyanie i problemy / /Kazakhstan-spektr. – 2005. – No.1. – p. 19.
10. Poslanie Prezidenta RK Nursultana Nazarbaeva narodu Kazakhstana "Strategiya vkhozhdeniya Kazakhstana v chislo pyatidesyati naibolee kokurentosposobnykh stran mira" / / Mysl. – 2006. – No.3, pp. 2-18.

3

Democracy in Central Asia

Kh. Umarov

INTRODUCTION

After the disintegration of the Soviet Union, many important socio-economic and political changes have taken place in the newly independent countries of Central Asia. Their state structure has undergone radical changes as compared to what existed during the Soviet times.

The main point is that all the five republics of Central Asia have become fully independent and have formed socio-political systems on their own without any interference from outside. In their very first declarations after independence, their leaders spoke about intentions of creating a democratic system, expansion of political rights of the people and introduction of elections for the basic elements of the state – the President, Parliament and judicial institutions.

Even during Soviet times, serious beginnings had been made to change the single-party system, and, soon after independence, a pluralist, multi-party political system began to develop in all the countries of this region. In Kazakhstan, Kyrgyzstan and Tajikistan, obstacles that stood in the way of setting up new political parties were removed. In Turkmenistan and Uzbekistan, it was a controlled process and new parties were allowed if they were helpful in promoting the interests of the dominant political elite.

In all countries of Central Asia, those leaders came to power who were already heading the Communist Parties of the time. It is no secret that the leaders of the Communist Parties were *de facto* controlling affairs of the states. Those leaders who had gone through hard political training during the Soviet times (I. Karimov, N. Nazarbaev and S. Niyazov) for a long time remained in power or continued after getting independence. But those leaders (M. Masaliev, R. Nabiev and K. Mahkamov) who came to power in the second half of Gorbachev's *perestroika* period could not hold on due to lack of experience. Leaders like A. Akaev and E. Rahmon replaced them.

In the initial years of independence in all the countries of Central Asia democratic liberties were declared; in particular, as: freedom of speech, freedom for holding meetings and freedom of conscience, etc. However, every country gave its own interpretation of the meaning and contents of democratic liberties. In Turkmenistan and Uzbekistan, though constitutional liberties existed formally, religious groups and mass media did not get the freedom to openly express their views. Even today, they are forced to reproduce only that information which does not go against official ideology and interests of the highest leadership of the country. Democratic liberties in Tajikistan, after E. Rahmon came to power, are getting restricted. Restrictions are being imposed in accordance with personal, clan and regional interests of the ruling elite. Public political meetings can be organized only with the permission of local authorities who generally refuse to give such permission. Kyrgyzstan is more liberal in this respect. However, in practice hardly any constructive purpose has been served by the freedom available in Kyrgyzstan.

In Kazakhstan, local authorities can give permission for holding public meetings and organizing processions. But, in practice, the critics of President Nazarbaev are persecuted, on insignificant grounds.

In Kyrgyzstan, certain restrictions have been imposed of late which have caused dissatisfaction among the people. In August 2008, the President approved new rules that placed restrictions on organizing processions and other political activities. The law prohibits holding mass meetings near 'strategic objects' like government offices, schools, higher educational institutions and major transport routes. According to human rights activists, local authorities are empowered to use new restrictions to disallow mass processions and other public meetings.[1]

In Uzbekistan, restrictions on democratic liberties are maximum. These have become more severe after the Andijon incidents. Uzbekistan is considered as one of the failed states and the world community cannot ignore the points that it is not prognessing on the path of democracy in a proper way. A large number of human rights activists and political prisoners are locked up in jails. Toshpulat Yuldashev, a well known political analyst of Uzbekistan who has been forced to live in exile is of the opinion that too much centralization and concentration of power in the hands of the President has turned Uzbekistan into a failed state. Such a situation has developed because the ruling elite is afraid of social unrest explosion that may occur as a result of polarization of Uzbek society since 5% of the population is in possession of 95% of its total resources.[2]

After the death of the first President of Turkmenistan, S. Niyazov–Turkmenbashi, who had put several restrictions on democratic freedoms and filled the jails with political prisoners, certain positive changes have started taking place in Turkmenistan. However, organization of processions and meetings against the policies of the government continue to be banned and any such attempt may invite punitive action from the security agencies. Turkmenistan is a country having, essentially, a single-party system. As a result, all political parties, except the President's party, have been paralyzed.

In Uzbekistan and Tajikistan ridiculous attempts are being made by the political leadership to set up 'puppet' parties. At the same time, all efforts are also being made to paralyze opposition parties. In Tajikistan, parallel parties with the same name are being created by openly bribing feeble opposition leaders. For this purpose, a well-tested but primitive mechanism is being used. For instance, a political party newly created by ruling circles approaches the court for recognition. The Ministry of Justice and the Court, on instructions from 'above', would give a decision in favour of the new puppet party and it get proper recognition. Then the real opposition party is declared out of bounds. In Tajikistan, just before the last Presidential elections, two new political parties – The Economic Development Party and The Agrarian Party came into existence on the initiative taken from 'above'. These parties were allowed to participate in the elections and even get some votes. After his triumphant victory in the elections, the present President thanked the leaders of these parties for their active participation in the elections.

Emergence of autocratic regimes is a common trend in all the countries of Central Asia and the ruling elites go on amending provisions of the Constitutions. They also blatantly misuse the administrative resources to create the most favourable conditions for themselves to get elected for a new term. During the parliamentary and presidential election campaigns, all the state structures and local organs of power are mobilised to vote in favour of the existing president. Opposition parties do not have such 'facilities'. After every parliamentary and presidential elections it has become very common for opposition parties to say that the results of the elections have been rigged.

The autocratic character of rule in the Central Asian countries is gradually leading to the growth of planting of personality cults around the presidents of these counties. Unlike the personality cult of Mao Zedong in China or Stalin, Khrushchev and Brezhnev in the erstwhile USSR, the personality cult in Central Asia is rather primitive in its character; from a modern angle it appears that the personality cult in these countries is odd and funny. For example, in Turkmenistan even the names of the days of week were changed and they were given new names of the closest relatives of the then President S. Niyazov. The new President of Turkmenistan has put an end to this absurdity.

The walls of skyscrapers, public buildings, offices of state functionaries are full of portraits and sayings of the leaders of these countries. In some, the main part of state television is devoted to the meetings, speeches and visits of their leaders. The programmes create the impression that negative phenomena like poverty, crime, prostitution, drug addiction, alcoholism and, drug trafficking do not exist.

As regards freedom of speech and freedom of the press, the situation is rather peculiar in Central Asia. In Kazakhstan, Kyrgyzstan and Tajikistan hundreds of new newspapers, magazines, radio and TV channels have come up. But the number of newspapers and magazines being printed is much less than number of copies during the Soviet period. A great majority of mass media in these countries are either private or corporate and they can hardly be called 'mass' media. Here, the main obstacle is finance. In most cases the mass media lacks its own financial sources. But some part is doing well. It is, however, no secret that such publications belong to family members of the ruling elite. One such person is the daughter of the President of Kazakhstan, Doriga Nazarbaeva who holds the largest mass media resources.

In Kazakhstan and Tajikistan the mass media does not permit, or almost does not permit, direct or indirect criticism of their top leaders. If any criticism does appear, then sanctions are imposed which outwardly do not seem to reflect an undemocratic attitude of the authorities. For instance, the tax inspectors will unearth some violation of tax regulations by the press where the magazines are printed. Quite obviously, other printing presses will come to know about this; and they will try to avoid printing of such newspapers and magazines. In Tajikistan, as a result of such obstructionist actions, two very popular newspapers, 'Nidon sukhan' and 'Ruzi nav', had to be closed down. It must be mentioned that the tax code of the Central Asian countries is such that all the tax payers could be violators of law. This peculiarity is used very cleverly by the ruling elite.

In Kazakhstan and Tajikistan what is permitted in the mass media is only controlled criticism of the top leadership. In essence, criticism of the president, his family members and persons close to him is not permissible. But one may criticize the activities of ministers, regional leaders and even the prime minister. In Kyrgyzstan, the situation in this regard seems to be a little better. But the print-run of publications, in particular non-government publications, is so small that the information fails to reach the masses.

In Uzbekistan and Turkmenistan the situation is worse. There is no transparency of information with regard to the ruling elite. It is just not possible to criticize the top persons of the state machinery. Any criticism may lead to unpleasant consequences for the author of the publication as well as the magazine, newspaper or television channel. Private publications are given access to the information space of these countries only when the responsible state organs are convinced about their loyalty to the ruling elite.

Thus, we see that though there is no Soviet-type censorship in the Central Asian countries, a sort of self-censorship is spreading more and more because political regimes of these countries are becoming increasingly authoritarian. Private newspapers, magazines and electronic media know very well that allowing any information that is unpleasant to the representatives of the political elite may lead to serious negative consequences.

Lack of democracy in the Central Asian countries, to a great extent, is due to the introduction of the Presidential system. The President enjoys very wide range of powers which are almost unlimited. This has led to the powers of Parliament, Government and regional organs of power getting reduced.

Parliaments have only a very limited influence on the democratic development of these countries because they themselves are subordinate to the President. They do not have the right to repeal the decrees of the President and to initiate the process of impeachment of the President. Democratic members of parliament are not in a position to exert any influence on decisions of national importance.

Such a situation is fraught with the danger that any initiative or proposal coming from the bottom is not likely to be implemented in practice. The efficiency of the state machinery depends on the desire of only one person – the Head of State. Sometimes, certain measures of national importance are taken at a lower level. For example, the President may ask the leader of parliament to pass the budget within a very short period of time; say, two days. This is done so as to bypass expression of dissatisfaction by the public regarding the revenues and propriety of expenditures from the state exchequer. In Tajikistan, Uzbekistan and Turkmenistan the budget process takes place in the usual manner through the lobbies of the state machinery. The public is not involved in its preparation, discussion and approval. In these countries, budget proposals are discussed by a committee of parliament for less than a day. There is no participation of the representatives of political parties, trade unions, representatives of NGOs and other components of civil society. There has been no response to requests made by academics and representatives of political parties to have a public discussion on the budget of the State.

In countries of Central Asia, self-permissiveness of the Presidents is getting manifested more and more. In Uzbekistan this was very clearly seen at the time of events in Andijon and after. Directions given by the President were taken as orders of an absolute monarch. Although the officially adopted documents give a formal permission, no one in this country has the right to object, reject or doubt any decision of the Head of State even if such decisions go against the basic interests of the peoples.

Going by his personal wishes, the President of Uzbekistan has been indulging in various manoeuvres at the international level; sometimes Uzbekistan gets closer to or sometimes it moves away from major powers. It has become a very common phenomenon for Uzbekistan to join or withdraw from regional blocks and organizations on the whims of the President. In these countries the Presidential system has been turned into Presidential self-permissiveness. Almost every important functionary is appointed by the Presidents: provincial public prosecutors, judges, vice chancellors and so on. One of the Presidents once said in public that Heads of Departments of higher educational institutions are also going to be appointed by him. Such an approach is undesirable because government servants become an object of purchase (The only exception is Kyrgyzstan where, after K. Bokiev came to power, only a few instances of self-permissiveness have been seen).

Transformation of democratic regimes into autocratic entities ones has come as a result of corruption in the higher echelons of power. Further, decisions of national importance are being taken on the basis of regionalism, localism and clan feelings. As these phenomena spread loyalties. The political elites of the region are inevitably driven to take measures restricting democratic liberties because the foundations of their rule may be shaken up.

The phenomena mentioned above are, leading to a slowdown of socio-economic development, increased poverty and migration. At present, migration of labour from Uzbekistan is 5.5 million persons, from Tajikistan the 1.5 million and from Kirgyzystan 0.8 million. The rate of migration is on the increase despite shortage of labour in the non-financial sector in these countries.

The analysis given here would indicate that the newly independent countries of Central Asia do require wide-ranging democratic reforms. Their economy is also in need of extensive democratization. Without such reforms it would not be possible to form a powerful middle class that could be the basis for political and social stability. Only then it would be possible to achieve a high level of economic and social growth, create a modern human capital and implement difficult structural changes to enable these countries to occupy a proper place in the world economy.

In this respect in recent years the countries of the European Union, OSCE and several international organizations, including NGOs have been undertaking activities successfully in Central Asian countries. It is hoped that these efforts will yield the desired results in the near future.

NOTES AND REFERENCES

1. *The Times of Central Asia,* August 14, 2008.
2. *The Times of Central Asia,* August 14, 2008.

4

Democracy and Security in Identity of Central Asia

Rustam Burnashev and Irina Chernykh

The present paper aims to discuss the place that the democracy and liberal values occupy in the models of identity being formed in countries of Central Asia. Our analysis is based on the example of Uzbekistan. Formation of identity (*I*) necessarily implies identification of one or more of the *Others*, who pose a threat to *I*. Any threat to identity coming from *Others* is not only something which is capable of destroying this identity; it is something which must be liquidated. From this point of view, questions of *security* are an ontological necessity for constructing the idea of identity.

1. IDENTITY AND SECURITY

In spite of criticism of the concept of *identity* (Brubaker and Cooper 2000), it is being used very actively and also effectively in structuralist and post-structuralist studies dealing with the question of formation of external, internal and security policies. The basic point of such studies is that policies depend upon the image of identity; and, at the same time, formulation of policy decides how identity is to be produced and reproduced. That is how *identification* takes place (Hansen 2006: 1). In this way, relations between identification, identity and policy are considered to be constitutive and performative. Identity is not something that the states, nations or other collective entities possess irrespective of practices of existing foreign or security policy (Katzenstein 1996). Separation of identity and policy is helpful in doing some analysis; however, it is to be noted that this separation does not necessarily reflect any specific process. The assumption that politicians make use of identity and, at the same time, form these identities is related to various conceptualizations of identity (Hansen 2006: 6).

Discursive Identity: There are no "objective" identities located in some extra-discursive sphere; what exists is only *identification* within the framework of discourse (text-process) and *identity* as a result of this identification (text-result). In such a case identity exists only to the extent that it re-articulates itself in a given discourse and does not face is competing discourse (Anderson 1983);

Political Identity: Within this discursive space there is production and reproduction of certain subjectivities and identities, along with and get suppression of other identifications;

Relative Identity: In a political discourse while articulating the identity of *I*, the identity of *Others* is also established. Thus, "a terrorist" can be identified only if he differs from "the freedom fighter" or "a soldier whose actions have been sanctioned by the state" (Der Derian 1992);

Social Identity: This is based on utilization of a set of collectively articulated codes. It is neither a personal birthright of an individual nor his psychological condition;

Thus, in the structuralist and post-structuralist approach to identity policy-deciding factors get articulated and at identities are produced and reproduced through these very political discourses.

2. DISCOURSE FORMATION

There are several methods of discourse analysis each of which is a sort of theoretical-methodological complex consisting of:

- philosophical concept of *discourse*;
- theoretical models;
- methodology of selecting the field of research[1];
- research technique.

Any discourse has its internal regularities and heterogeneities. By studying these regularities and heterogeneities it is possible to know how a discourse is composed and what is the logic of its structure or code.

Yet, discourse analysis leaves many questions unanswered. For instance, it does not aim to find out and, reveal the conditions and rules of functioning and transformation of a discourse. While the concept of *discourse* refers to a resultant text, *discourse practice* signifies the process of formation and use (perception and interpretation) of a discourse. Discourse pre-supposes a structure (a code), and discourse practice pre-supposes certain *rules*.

An important aspect of the idea of discourse practice is its unity or cohesion as it tries to answer the question – Are there any dominant set of rules in the given space which determine the contours of discussion of any problem? Or whether in the given space co-existence of several discourse practices are possible?

We adhere to the position of M. Foucault that each age has its own set of rules. The discourse space is formed as one whole in which every sign is fixed as a moment by means of its relations to other signs. This is achieved by excluding all other possible meanings of the signs. However, we think that in the discourse space it is possible to make distinction between levels or layers (O. Wæver 2002; 2005). At higher layers while a given identity is preserved, one can observe certain differences of discourse practices and discourses. By following E. Laclau and Ch. Mouffe (1985), we may talk about a pluralistic concept of discourse in which discourse practices struggle with each other for establishing supremacy in the discourse space.

The space occupied by the structural unity of discourses and discourse practices peculiar to a particular age is called *discourse formation*. The discourse formation determines what can be said or heard and by whom, and what cannot be said. "One cannot speak of anything at any time" (Foucault 1972: 44). In other words, it is the *structural conditions of existence* which determine discourse structure and rules. They decide about the sense of something on which utterances are significant in a given discourse formation. These conditions are historical in character. As such, those categories and arguments which are effective in some period and place may sound senseless or absurd in some other time or space.

We may say that the question of significance,[2] i.e. (how and why some utterances are taken to be serious) is central to the understanding of discourse formation. Acceptance of an utterance as significant is supported by a whole network of relations of power which is determined by the rules of discourse formation as well as its structure.

- what is being said; the concepts (*words*) which are acceptable in a given formation;
- subject of the utterance;
- who makes the utterance;
- theories of discourse (e.g., classical or non-classical approach).

3. ANALYSIS OF DISCOURSE FORMATION

From our point of view the most effective method by which we can examine discourse formation is archaeology,[3] as proposed and developed by M. Foucault.

Problematization

According to M. Foucault problematization originates when incongruity is revealed between speaking and seeing. In order "to see" this incongruity, one has to do something like archaeological aloofness.[4]

In our study the key task is to decide how "national security" is emerging as a dominant form of politics and security in countries of Central Asia? How "stability" is becoming so much important for understanding what is meant by Kazakhstan, Uzbekistan or Tajikistan politically. What are the forms of problematization, what are the networks of relations between what is being said and what is being seen which have made this possible.

Diagnosis of discourse formation

After problematizing, the discourse formation which is to be studied, archaeology starts 'a *pure description of discursive events*' (Foucault 1972: 27), i.e. Archaeology describes and registers a closed set of means of dealing with utterances which are manifested in the formation being studied. In this regard, the description of discourse formation is directed towards determining how its objects, subjects, concepts and theories are formed.

Determining the Structure and Rules of Discourse Formation

While describing a discourse formation it is necessary to find out the *structural conditions* which determine its existence and value-relations that are inherent in it, its rules of practices and structure.

A discourse is formed by fixation of meanings around some nodal points (Laclau and Mouffe 1985: 112); there are signs around which other signs are organized. The set of nodal points may consist of only one concept. For example, S. Abashin (2002) mentions the concept of *regionalism* as the key concept while describing the Tajik Conflict of the 1990s, or a set of concepts (O. Wæver 2005) like *state* and *nation.*

In the beginning of the 20th century, the nodal points of the discursive space of Central Asia were determined within the framework of the Soviet Union. Great unprecedented efforts were made to institutionalize and codify what is meant by "national" (Brubaker 1996). The territory of the Soviet Union was divided into more than 50 formally autonomous national formations each related to a certain ethnic group. Every citizen was given an ethnic identity based on origin and the ethnic identity was registered in identification documents. "In doing so, the regime was not simply *recognizing* or *ratifying* a pre-existing state of affairs; it was *newly constituting* both persons and places *as national*" (Brubaker and Cooper 2000: 26).

With the disintegration of USSR, in formation of modern States[5] became a possibility and; there arose the necessity of forming national and state identities. Such questions were put in very clear terms: what is the original territory of each nation and; what should be the state structure of each nation; how the national language should develop, what should be its status and relationship with the Russian language, what should be the national symbols and what should be the role of the intelligentsia. The categories of *state* and *nation* became the central theme of national discourse in countries of the region.

If *state* and *nation* are to be the nodal points of discursive space, it is necessary to decide: who is the meaningful 'speaker' in this space. Here we notice a sort of asymmetry. If the state is legitimate by itself, then the nation never speaks; it is manifested in what is said by others on its behalf. Traditionally, it is the state which speaks on behalf of a nation. Moreover, the modern state has been one of the most important agents of identification and categorization, which has monopolised the power and right to decide what is what and who is who (Brubaker and Cooper 2000: 15). The identification as pursued by the state can be examined in at least two ways:

fixation and collection of individual markers (e.g., making of passports, collection of finger-prints, photographs and signatures);

classification of citizens on the basis of sex, religion, property, ethnicity and literacy through census.

These methods of individualization and collectivization are the central point of the phenomenon of *governmentality* of a modern State (Foucault 1991).

Of course, there are other structures, institutions or personalities who can speak on behalf of the nation and sub-national communities. They can even get some support for a certain period of time. However, their legality as representatives of society would always be in doubt.

The State – Nation Linkage

O. Wæver (2002: 35-37) says that, while studying what the idea of a state is, what the idea of a nation is and how they are related with each other, it is necessary:

a. to examine whether a country forms its identity around a stable cohesion of nation and state, or whether nation and state are independent of each other.[6]
b. to decide how a nation is formed: does one belong to a nation depending upon culture, language and birth; or it is a political construct which, in principle, is open to newly assimilated members;
c. to examine how the idea of the state is constructed by external and internal dimensions: the external dimension concerns projecting the state to the world;
d. the internal dimension in concerns projecting of the idea of state to the electorate, as a public welfare state, a socialist state or a liberal-capitalist state.
e. to reveal the presence of 'appendages' to the idea of a nation and,
f. to reveal the presence of "linking concepts" which can describe the relations between the state and the nation or the nation and its 'appendages'.

Wæver talks about two "ideal types" for the construction of the nation-state: the French and German models.

The French model "consists of a *fusion* of state and nation, in a mutually constitutive relationship (Wæver 2002: 34). A nation is defined in relation to state and, at the same time, it forms the basis of the state. This construction is known as the 'Western' type of national identity or "political (civil)" national identity. The French model includes two more elements: necessity of the external European role and necessity of the concept of Fatherland (the *patrie*) which form the basis of the nation (Wæver 2002: 34).

In the German model, nation and state exist as two leading ideas which can be combined as well as contrasted; "the nation is culture, the state is power" (Wæver 2005: 46). Germany was formed on the experience of absence of unity as a state whereas nation was in existence. The German concept of state was formed by the fact that its object did not exist, it was something which had to be created in a clearly inimical atmosphere. That is why when the German state began to take shape in the 19th century, its main functions were the struggle for power and external self-expression. In this way, the German and as the French states played an external role. For a very long time, the German nation existed outside the state. "In contrast to the French nation, which is constituted by the state – and is simultaneously the foundation for the state – the German nation exists in itself as an ethno-cultural phenomenon." (Wæver 2005: 46). The German construction can be called as an *ethnic type* of national identity.

The Linkage of "I" and the "Others"

The identification of the national *I* pre-supposes the identification of one or more of the *Others* whose identity differs from the identity of *I* and who pose a threat to *I* by their very existence (Campbell 1992: 55). Here *I* and the series of *Others* are not just simply oppositions; they are constructive oppositions. A threat to the security of the state coming from the *Others* is not only something which has the potential to undermine the state, it is something which must be liquidated. From this point of view, security is an ontological necessity for the state, not because the state has to be protected from threats but because its identity depends upon them.

The identity of the state is organized in two ways:

- separation of the internal sphere from the international;
- outlining internal *Others*.

There are three points relevant to the construction of identity in the discourse of security (Hansen 2006: 37-38):

a. The correlation *I - Others* may cover several levels of otherness ranging from the functional differences to individual non-correspondences: spatial, temporal, political. Thus, along with radical and threatening opposition more complex constructions of differences can also be mentioned:
   - identities striving to go beyond the limits of the existing radical opposition;
   - identities striving to integrate the existing opposition or their elements;
   - identities which articulate the *Others* as superior to *I* or identical with it.
b. The construction of identity includes, a series of oppositions consisting of several different *Others.* That is why it is also important to study how the differences amongst various *Others* are established and how such differences undergo change in time.
c. Identification always takes place in some spatial, temporal and ethical dimensions situation. An analysis of the method by which these three dimensions are connected with each other, would expand the basis for the study of subjects like security.

DISCOURSE FORMATION IN CENTRAL ASIA

In Central Asia, the concepts of *state* and *nation* emerged in the beginning of the 20th century.[7] There was no experience of either the state or the nation. As such, it was a "quasi-statehood".

The situation had changed in the 1990s when modern states were born in Central Asia. However, this was also the time when the category of *elite*[8] was added to the State and Nation. This category is taken to be the main organising actor which strives to overcome or compensate the limited power of the acting which characterized the Soviet period. Analysis of the ideas of state and nation needs to be supplemented with an analysis of the elite. It is necessary to study whether the combination of state, nation and elite would be stable. Secondly, can the elite be considered homogenous. Unlike the French and German models, nation and state in Central Asia have been created by elites; and, it is the elites who are occupying the position of significant speaker (and, listener too).[9] Here the state, was related not to the political concept of a nation but to the cultural-ethnic concept, the concept of a *titular nation*.[10] Moreover, the state itself acquired an ethnic dimension and became ethnocratic. Accordingly, *Others* also got structured as something different from the elite, the state and / or nation-culture (the ethnos).

Thus, the *first layer* of discourse formation in Central Asia is the linkage 'elite – state – nation-culture (ethnos)' which is correlated with the construction of *Others* and which obtains its ultimate basis in the concept of independence.

The elite which forms the state (accordingly, equating itself to the state or putting itself above it) and the ethnos get the right to long-term legitimacy which is ensured through the idea of *stability*. Moreover, the elite occupying such a position finds enough basis for presenting itself as an object whose existence must be preserved; and, it should have the right to decide on threats to national and state security. The elite that is constructed as "not replaceable" even within democratic procedures. It is not liable to be criticised even within liberal procedures because it would wash away the "unity" of the nation and the state. In this way, security and stability are contrasted with democracy and freedom.

The state which is constructed with the ideas of security and stability tends to acts as a suppressing force in external as well as internal matters. Huge resources are spent in dealing with internal politics to ensure stability of the regime.

The identity built on the linkage elite – state – national-culture-security (ethnos) gives rise to, at least, three constructions:

nation-state-national culture (ethnos);
elite – the state; and,
nation-culture (ethnos).

Through this linkage with security the *second layer* of discourse formation is formed with *stability and security/ democracy and freedom* as nodal points.

In the *third layer* the specific objects and subjects of archaeological deconstruction are formed.

At this level it would be more effective if we concentrate our analysis on one of the countries of Central Asia. As an example, we shall take the case of Uzbekistan.

Uzbekistan, as an independent state, has passed through four phases:

Phase of uncertainty and struggle for power (1988-1993);

Phase of building up of the state and concentration on traditional threats to security (1993-1998);

Phase of concentration on "new dimensions of security" (1998-2003);

Phase of threat from the "Colour Revolutions" (2003 onwards).

In the competing discourses in Uzbekistan during 1988-1993, the concept of the titular nation was considered as indisputable, and the linkages "state – nation-culture (ethnos)" and "elite – nation-culture (ethnos)", were not challenged. The understanding of the linkage "elite – state" was differentiated along four lines leading to the emergence of *nationalist, religious, democratic* and *state* discourses vying with each other. The ruling party-*nomenklatura* elite of Uzbekistan was trying to strengthen its influence by forming ethnocratic secular statehood (the Turkish model) with clear orientation towards etatism, leading role of the bureaucracy and personification of power (projecting a national charismatic leader) and also by compromising with opposition forces. Building up of the state in this manner provided a legitimate opportunity to the ruling circles of Uzbekistan to modernise the structure of the Soviet, power step-by-step. The transformation took place without any difficulty because the proposed model of rule matched with the views of the bureaucracy and the thinking of a major part of the indigenous population which associated this type of rule with ideas of *orderliness* and *social justice*. At the same time, in the beginning of 1990s tensions grew between local inhabitants and the sub-ethnic groups of the local bureaucracy. Re-traditionalization, along with cultivation of relations based on subordination of the individual to the collective, led to a revival of clan and religious structures and shifting of economic and political questions to sub-state centres of power.[11] As in Tajikistan, these tendencies in combination with the socio-economic crisis prompted the lower-ranked groups to struggle for a change in the balance which was in favour of the elites.

In the middle of 1990s the ruling bureaucratic elite, was able to establish control over the situation and significantly limit the activities of opposition groups by putting stress on the security of the "state – nation-culture (ethnos)". Stability is declared as a fundamental values and for its sake it is worthwhile to forego some of the democratic and liberal values. The Civil War in Tajikistan showed the way to Uzbekistan that, along with religious extremism and fundamentalism, it was equally necessary to pay special attention to the clan and religious structure of the country (Karimov 1998). Establishment of a strong Presidential system in Uzbekistan was a reflection of the requirements of the national elite to consolidate and strengthen its influence under conditions of a new model of social development. Stress was also laid on traditional threats to security and the possibility of interference by neighbouring regional powers or a new 'Great Game' (Karimov 1998). A new concept of "non-constructive opposition" was introduced "which under the banner of democracy and by its actions has provoked destabilization of society" and "has been pursuing clan and localistic aims" (Karimov 1998: 126, 141). The main nodal points of the competing discourses during this period were preservation of the values of the country and liberalization.

At the end of the 1990s and beginning of 2000 relations between the states of Central Asia and the personified ruling bureaucratic elite became so strong that the ruling elites began to put emphasis on the security of "the state – ruling elite" in countries of Central Asia and enforced changes in the constitutional structure. For the first time in the political discourse "new dimensions of security" came to occupy a premier position with stress being laid on their "external" origin. Changes in threat perception and expansion of the concept of security is reflected in the Acts passed in Uzbekistan and in the concept documents: The Concept of National Security (1987), The Defence Doctrine (2000), and The Defence Act (2001).[12] In accordance with such the threats, reforms with power structure started taking place. The opposition forces which were thrown out of the political process and transformed into *Others* are in favour of preserving the constitution structure. They are of the opinion that Karimov being the President is a violation of the Constitution of the country and, therefore, it is not legitimate. The nodal points of the competing discourses during this period are: *preservation of constitutional structure* and *illegitimacy of the personified ruling elite.*

In the mid-2000, the impact of the wave of democratization of the post-Soviet space got support from the Georgia ("Rose Revolution" of 2003) and Ukraine ("the Orange Revolution" of 2004). In Uzbekistan there was talk of the threat of loss of specific national character which could occur from accelerated democratization and liberalization being forced from outside. The events of 2005 in Kyrgyzstan are a clear example of *destabilization* being an unavoidable consequence of the "Colour Revolutions".

Stress was being laid on the security of "elite – nation-culture (ethnos)". International terrorism, religious extremism and new structures like NGOs and various Funds began to be cited as players which had provided the text for the discourse on security in Uzbekistan. Now the competing nodal points were *evolutionary development of the state* and *democratization through revolution*. However, the dominant discourse 'gets divided into' several parts which, were mostly repetition of points of the earlier periods.

An overview of security discourse formation in Uzbekistan is presented in Figure 1.

	1993-1998	1998-2003	2003 onwards
Threats	Traditional threats: destabilization; Afghanization/ Tajikization	New dimensions of security. religious extremism; international terrorism	Colour Revolutions: destabilization; loss of specific national features
Layer 3	Maintenance of integrity of the country vs. liberalization	Preservation of constitutional set-up vs Illegitimacy of the personified ruling elite	Evolutionary development of the state vs democratization through revolution
Layer 2	Security of the state – nation-culture (ethnos)	Security of the elite – the state	Security of the elite – the nation-culture (ethnos)
Layer 1	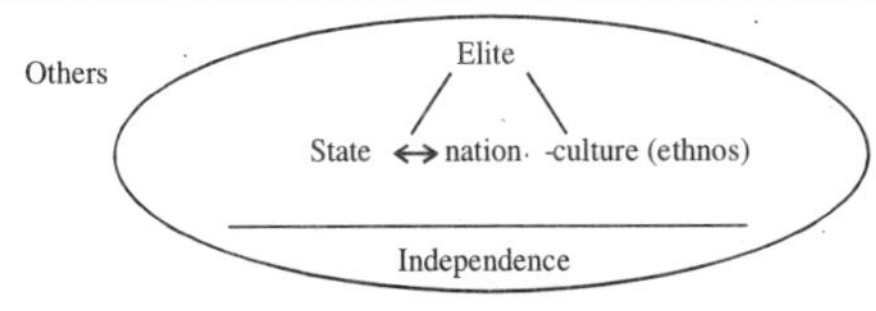		

Figure 1: Security Discourse in Uzbekistan (end of 1980s to the middle of 2000s)

It is clear that, in Central Asia, formation of states has taken place with the central ideas of security and stability. Security of the ruling elite being the main concern issue before these states, a significant part of resources is directed towards of internal politics in order to ensure the stability of the regime. On the whole, the structure of discourse formation is constructed by constructing *identity* and its separate components (elite – state – nation-culture) and perceptions of *stability/democracy* and *security/freedom*.

NOTES AND REFERENCES

1. The present study is based on two types of texts:
   - texts which have been authored by politicians, primarily by the President of Uzbekistan I.Karimov;
   - texts authored by Uzbek scholars, analysts and journalists.
2. According to the terminology of H. Dreyfus è P. Rabinow (1983: 48) – this is a question of serious speech act. Seriousness is contrasted with *laughter* with which the work of M. Foucault *Words and Things* begins, - "the laughter that shattered ... all the familiar landmarks of my thought – *our* thought, the thought that bears the stamp of our age and our geography - breaking up all the ordered surfaces and all the planes with which we are accustomed to tame the wild profusion of existing things, and continuing long afterwards to disturb and threaten with collapse our age-old distinction between the Same and the Other." (Foucault 1970: xv).
3. Choice of archaeology as a method of studying discourse formations is important in the sense that archaeology itself does not take meaningful (serious) utterances seriously and belongs to the group of "funny sciences (la gaya scienza" (Burnashev 2000, 2002). Reconstructions of archaeological method are given in the works of Dreyfus and Rabinow (1983), Deleüze (1988), Kendal and Wickham (1999).
4. Spontaneous reflection of such aloofness is *laughter* (see Endnote 13).
5. For the concepts of pre-modernist, modernist and post-modernist states, see, for example: Caporoso (1996); Cooper (1996); Buzan and Segal (1996).
6. When state and nation do not coincide, as for example, when there are a substantial number of sub-national communities ("national minorities"), then increase in the level of security of these communities shall partly decrease the security of the state. Thus, if the state is implementing some homogenizing "national " programme, then its security will come in conflict with the security of "national" projects of the sub-communities.
7. See S.Abashin (2004).
8. Use of the term *elite* contains in itself a quite serious threat of reductionism: the elite can be taken to be a definite and clearly structured subject, a sort of "collective personality" which encourages others to follow simplified descriptive and explicative models (Osipov 2004: 210). It is important to note that the term "elite" is applied to discourse practice in the sense of a concept, and also to non-discourse practice, therby meaning some institution. It is this ambiguity which leads to the efforts to objectivize the elite.
9. There is no doubt that it is not sufficient to say that the concepts of the nation and the state in Central Asia and Kazakhstan have

been created by the elite. It equally necessary to answer some other questions: How did this project, after all, succeed? How did the people react to these "created" identities and what happened to the self-consciousness of the society? What is the mechanism of accepting identities?

10. In the Soviet Union a *titular nation* was understood as an *ethnic group* and its name was the deciding factor in the official naming of a territory or quasi-state formation (union republic, autonomous republic, autonomous region, autonomous district). A titular nation had a privileged position in comparison with other ethnic groups – they got some concessions in admission to educational institutions (the so-called "national cadres"), the languages and cultures of titular nations got support from the state, and a local 'nomenklatura' was formed out of the representatives of the titular nation. In this way, titular groups had a feeling of right to property within a certain territory, and to a great extent self-rule (if not autonomy) was legitimized. With passage of time marginalization of other *non-titular* ethnic groups started taking place who were looked upon as outsiders or immigrants irrespective of the history of their settlement in a given territory.
11. "Tradition", "clan", "regional structures" etc should not be taken as certain non-historical entities – these concepts emerge at a particular time in the language of the elite and experts, their meanings go on changing, and relations of dominance are established with their help.
12. The Concept of National Security of the Republic of Uzbekistan (1997) and the Defence Doctrine of the Republic of Uzbekistan (2000) are confidential documents (the first document bears the stamp "For Official Use", and the second document bears the stamp "Secret"). For the text of the Act of Defence see 'Act of the Republic of Uzbekistan, dated 3 July 1992 "On Defence" as amended by the Act of 11 May 2001'. *Vedomosti Olii Majlisa Respubliki Uzbekistan*, 2001, 5, p. 80.

BIBLIOGRAPHY

(A) Russian

Abashin, Sergei (2002): "Regionalizm v Tajikistane: stanovlenie "etnicheskogo yazyka" in Oksana Karpenko, Aleksandr Osipov and Viktor Voronkov (Eds.), *Rasizm v yazyke sotsialmnykh nauk*, St.Petersburg: Aleteiya, 70-93.

Abashin, Sergei (2004): Naselenie Ferganskoi doliny, in Sergei Abashin, Valentin Bushkov (Eds.), *Ferganskaya dolina: etnichnost, etnichweskie protsessy, etnicheskie konflikty*, Moscow: Nauka: 38-101.

Burnashev, Rustam (2000): '"La Gaya Scienza": invariantny ideal nauki', *Vestnik Kazakhskogo gosudarstvennogo universiteta im. al Farabi. Seriya 'Filosofiya, Kulturologiya, Politilogiya'*, No.1 (13).

Burnashev, Rustam (2002): '"La Gaya Scienza": fenomenologiya', *Vestnik Kazakhskogo gosudarstvennogo universiteta im. al Farabi. Seriya 'Filosofiya, Kulturologiya, Politilogiya'*, No.1 (15).

Karimov, Islam (1998): 'Uzbekistan na poroge XXI veka: ugrozy bezopasnosti, usloviya i garantii progressa', in Islam Karimov, *Po puti bezopasnosti i stabilnogo razvitiya,* Tashkent: Uzbekiston: 29-244.

Osipov, Aleksandr (2004): 'Ferganskie sobytiya 1989 goda (konstruirovanie etnicheskogo konflikta', in Serfei Abashin and Vitalii Bushkov (Eds.), *Fergaskaya dolina: etnichnost, etnichweskie protsessy, etnicheskie konflikty,* Moscow: Nauka: 164-223.

(B) English

Anderson, Benedict (1983): *Imagined Communities: Reflections on the Origin and Spread of Nationalism,* 2nd ed., London: Vero

Brubaker, Roger (1996): *Nationalism Reframed,* Cambridge

Brubaker Rogers and Frederick Cooper (2000): 'Beyond "Identity"', *Theory and Society,* 1: 1-47.

Buzan, Barry and Gerald Segal (1996): 'The Rise of the "Lite" Powers: A Strategy for Postmodern States', *World Policy Journal* 13 (3): 1-10

Campbell, David (1992): *Writing Security: United States: Foreign Policy and the Politics of Identity,* Manchester: Manchester University Press

Caporoso, James (1996): 'The European Union and Forms of the State: Westphalian, Regulatory or Post-Modern?', *Journal of Common Market Studies* 34 (1): 29-52

Cooper, Robert (1996): *The Postmodern State and the World Order,* London: Demos Paper no 19

Deleuze, Gilles (1988): *Foucault,* Minneapolis: University of Minnesota Press

Der Derian, James (1992): *Antidiplomacy: Spies, Terror, Speed, and War,* Oxford: Basil Blackwell

Dreyfus, Hubert L., and Paul Rabinow (1983): *Michel Foucault. Beyond Structuralism and Hermeneutics,* 2nd ed., Chicago: The University of Chicago Press

Foucault, Michel (1970): *The Order of Things: An Archaeology of the Human Sciences,* London: Tavistock Publications

Foucault, Michel (1972): *The Archaeology of Knowledge,* London: Tavistock Publications

Foucault, Michel (1991): 'Governmentality', in Graham Burchell et al. (eds.), *The Foucault Effect: Studies in Governmentality,* Chicago: The University of Chicago Press, 87-104

Hansen, Lene (2006): *Security as Practice: Discourse Analysis and the Bosnian War*, London: Routledge

Katzenstein, Peter (ed.) 1996: *The Culture of National Security: Norms and Identity in World Politics*, New York: Columbia University Press

Kendal, Gavin, and Gary Wickham (1999): *Using Foucault's Methods*, London, SAGE Publications

Laclau, Ernesto and Chantal Mouffe (1985): *Hegemony and Socialist Strategy: Towards a Radical Democratic Politics*, London: Verso

Wæver, Ole (2002): 'Identity, Communities and Foreign Policy: Discourse Analysis as Foreign Policy Theory', in Lene Hansen and Ole Wæver (eds.), *European Integration and National Identity: The Challenge of the Nordic States*, London and New York, Routledge, 20-49

Wæver, Ole (2005): 'European Integration and Security: Analysing French and German Discourses on State, Nation and Europe', in David Howarth and Jacob Torfing (eds.), *'Discourse Theory in European Politics: Identity, Policy and Governance'*, New York: Palgrave Macmillan: 33-67

5

The Growth of Democracy in Kazakhstan

K.N. Makasheva

INTRODUCTION

Till today, there is no common view in the social discourse about the optimum form of political organization of non-western societies. The Russian scholar A. Volodin has noted that "The modern reality of democratisation with all its complexities is far ahead of the theory of democracy."

The concept of a non-liberal democracy which was put forward towards the end of the 1980s was promoted officially by USA. The United States, in fact, recognized the possibility of existence of special models of democracy for countries of the Middle East; and, hence, for all countries with non-western political traditions.

Today we can talk about diversification of democracy in the conscious absence of uniform political reforms in countries of the post-Soviet space. The question is: How are questions of democratisation perceived in these countries?

Firstly, the question of the development of institutions of a democratic society in Kazakhstan is one of the hottest topics among professionals; it is also discussed widely in the media, during election campaigns, and when burning political questions are taken up. Yet, there is no common understanding of the term "democratisation of society". A large part of the political class is of the opinion that civil society is one of the main attributes of democratic system, thereby meaning the maximum involvement of common people in the political process; and, first of all, in the election process.

At the same time, there is another equally widespread view of democratisation amongst the 'humanitarian' intelligentsia who identify democratic principles of civil society with the pre-revolutionary concept of 'society' which was the key concept in Russian liberal consciousness towards the end of the 19th and beginning of the 20th century. Society is the bearer of democratic ideals and stands in contrast to bureaucratic rule which became aloof to the needs of the common people.

In such a paradigm, democratic processes are contrasted against the bureaucratic machinery of the state which has moved away from reality. As far as the "classical" understanding of a democratic, civil society is concerned whose citizens as a community live with observance of rules, and supremacy of law, it can be said that consistent supporters of a civil society in Kazakhstan have lived well less than what they expected. However, to comprehend the situation is not so much unambiguous, it is necessary to examine more carefully what this formula interns.

Secondly, democracy, in the sense of "peoples rule" expects every member of society to be an active, with involvement in the political process and knowledge of its main participants. This is necessary for making a conscious choice in favour of a political party or some programme of action. In the United States the average citizen knows the names of Senators from their state, of country judge and the Sheriff of the town. On the other hand, in the post-Soviet space, political absenteeism is very large.

Thirdly, it is important to consider the social component of democratisation. Civil society cannot afford to be polarized in social stratification. The middle class forms the basis of democracy and civil society. In spite of being non-homogenous, it traditionally gives preference to political representation than to any other form of rule, and it favours evolutionary changes. That is why in the political systems outside Western political traditions, only a powerful middle class can form the basis for real institutionalization of democracy.

After the disintegration of the Soviet Union 18 years ago, Kazakhstan declared its independence and sovereignty. Independence was the first step for resurgence provided a historical opportunity for the rebirth of statehood, and solve problems accumulated during the previous regime. It was only after independence that it was possible to decide on vital issues like closure of the Semipalatinsk nuclear test site, to start serious economic reforms, liquidate sharp structural imbalances in the economy and to utilize the natural resources of the country for welfare. Independence made it possible to revive the Kazakh language and traditional culture. Kazakhstan is now full-fledged member of the world community and has been able to create a favourable international climate, establish cooperation in political, economic and cultural fields with leading countries of the world. Major international initiatives have been reflected in the Address of the President Nazarbaev entitled "A New Kazakhstan in the New World".[1] The future of any country is built upon three pillars – a legitimate state, market economy and democracy. The Constitution of Kazakhstan has clearly set the following aims: affirmation of Kazakhstan as a democratic, secular, legitimate and social state whose highest values are basic human, rights and freedom.[2]

Central Asia has as their neighbours the two largest populated countries of the world – India and China. Both are developing at a very fast pace. The expected growth of these two countries will also depend upon our attitude towards them.

In terms of territory, Kazakhstan is the biggest republic in Central Asia. It is rich in natural resources and has a bright economic future. At the same time, one cannot ignore the varied ethnic and religious composition of the Kazakh society and the disproportion between its area which is equivalent to Western Europe and the population of 15 million. These factors make Kazakhstan vulnerable to external forces.

Right from the time of its independence, Kazakhstan has pursued stable development. In economics, its natural resources are a dominant factor. Kazakhstan is the uncontested leader in chromites having one-third of the world's deposits. It has the second largest deposits of uranium. In copper, manganese and zinc its position is fourth; in deposits of lead and iron its position is sixth; in cobalt it is seventh; in coal and gold eighth; in aluminum tenth; and, in nickel its position is twelfth.[3]

Kazakhstan has taken a number of steps in integrating with the world community. One such step is to declare itself as a non-nuclear state. In fact, interest of other countries in Kazakhstan was not only due to its advantageous geopolitical location and natural resources. It had inherited from the erstwhile USSR the fourth most powerful arsenal of nuclear arms, and 104 SS-14 missiles with 1216 warheads. That is why, in 1991 itself the Secretary of

State James Baker, Prime Minister Margaret Thatcher and the Foreign Minister of FRG, Hans Dietrich Genscher paid visits to Almaty. They wanted Kazakhstan to give up this heritage in retain for a guarantee of security and financial compensation. In his book "Epicentre of the World", President Nazarbaev recalls the arguments for retaining these weapons:

> The nuclear umbrella by itself serves as a sort of guarantee of security and restrains the ambitions of any possible opponent. In the opinion of the authors of such arguments, retention of nuclear strength could compensate for qualitative and quantitative gaps in conventional arms and ammunitions. It was also argued that with its nuclear weapons, Kazakhstan could be a regional super-power. But Kazakhstan was able to get guarantees of nuclear security from the Permanent Members of the Security Council. Western powers also gave the green signal to business circles for cooperation with Kazakhstan. In this way, Kazakhstan got the benefits of a number of programs which gave it access to technical, organisational and financial help from specialized international structures like the IMF, World Bank and EBRD.[4]

India's geographical area is seventh largest in the world and its population is second largest. It has a bourgeois-parliamentary regime with democratic fundamentals. Democracy lives along with very old historical and cultural traditions. This has evoked special interest in Western and Russian scholars. According to the US historian E.T. Embry, the beginnings of democracy in India go back to the 1880s when, interactions between the British rulers and traditional Indian systems, led to the formation of a society with structural properties typical of contemporary Western states. Actually, Indian society had inherent qualities conducive to democratic tendencies and political modernization which helped in the establishment of a civil society of a specific type. The national freedom movement of India under the leadership of Mahatma Gandhi and Jawaharlal Nehru had parliamentary democracy, human rights, freedom and promotion of the interests of the oppressed classes as main political elements in the anti-colonial struggle.

The system of parliamentary representative democracy has been existing in India for more than half a century with its highly diverse economic, ethno-national, socio-cultural and other relations. Since 1990s various economic reforms have been carried out in

India in order to modernize the industry, reduce inflation, encourage private business activities and attract foreign capital investments.

India has been showing interest in strengthening its relations with the Central Asian States (CAS) for a number of reasons. Though India and the CAS are not neighbours, they are closely connected by historical ties, trade and economic relations.

India in the CAS is interested in political stability, economic growth, democracy values, independence and reduce the possibility of being manipulated by external forces. For India, it does not matter which model these countries will adopt for their development and what would be the role of Islam in their political and cultural life.

The policy of Islamization that is being followed by countries of Central Asia is, on the whole, likely to strengthen Islamists in the region and promote and activate fundamentalist and separatist movements in the Muslim population of India. That is why the Indian leaders have expressed the hope that the CAS would follow the principles of secularism, pluralism and democracy.

The world community looks upon India as the largest and strongest democracy which has followed secularism and social justice as state policy. Through Non-Aligned Movement, India has played a leading role in establishment of close relations with the Third World and one of the Super Powers – the erstwhile Soviet Union. Finally, the pursuit of economic reforms from the 1990s has had a decisive effect on the role and place of India in the modern world.

In the new millennium India is in the list of ten major economies of the world with a GDP of US $ 600 billion in the year 2004. The tempo of growth of the economy was maintained even during difficult climate conditions of the 1995-1996 and 1997-1998; and at the time of the Asian financial crisis of the same period. Delhi was also able to withstand the fallout of the international sanctions imposed on it after it conducted nuclear tests in 1998. Moreover, it is projected that by 2020, India's GDP would exceed the GDP of France by two times; and by the year 2035 it would surpass the GDP of Japan. In other words, India is likely to become third most powerful economy of the world after China and USA.[5]

Kazakhstan and India are multi-religious, multi-lingual and multi-cultural. Both are secular and committed to peaceful methods for solving differences. Views of the two countries also coincide in realization of the objectives of the Conference on Interactions and Confidence Building Measures in Asia (CICA) and the Congress of World and Traditional Religions whose initiative was taken by President Nazarbaev in 2003. The Ambassador of India to Kazakhstan, Ashok Mukherjee has pointed out that mutual understanding and mutual support in bilateral and international relations is, to a great extent, due to the good connections between the peoples of these two countries.[6]

India's experience in the fight against terrorism, religious extremism and separatism is of great practical significance for Kazakhstan. Taking into account the role and significance of India in the contemporary world, Kazakhstan supports the candidature of India for being elected as a permanent member of the UN Security Council. Kazakhstan has welcomed the decision taken at the Summit Meeting of Heads of States of the Shanghai Cooperation Organization to give the Observer status to India. Kazakhstan side has taken the position that India would be able to give additional impetus to the activities of SCO, in particular in regional economic cooperation.

The process of democratization and development of civil society in Kazakhstan is proceeding smoothly and gradually. Yet, it is not practically possible "to measure" it quantitatively.

Formation of civil society is a necessary step in real democratisation. In the post-Soviet space, the process of formation of civil society and the process of democratisation would be going to different from the classical Western model. It will depend upon the prevailing environment and political stability. In this respect formation of a powerful middle class would be a necessary pre-condition. Therefore, the path chosen by Kazakhstan, the path of democratization through economic modernization, seems to be the correct path. President Nazarbaev has always emphasized a change from the economic component to political democracy is the most appropriate approach.[7]

For establishing a real democracy, it is necessary to ensure that the institutions of civil society are integrated into the economic and socio-political processes first. It is also necessary to ensure that all layers of society get harmonized around the reforms.

Kazakhstan has gone through various stages and models of political stabilization. After utilizing the potential of one model, it was replaced by a new one. At present the search is for an optimal stabilization model, the so-called Kazakh model.

The first stage from 1991-1995 saw 'real' independence and adoption of the Constitution of sovereign Kazakhstan. During this period, attention was paid to arrest the disintegration processes, lay the foundation of Kazakhstan's statehood, move to political pluralism and create the foundations for democratic development.

The second stage from 1995-2000 was devoted to creation and strengthening of modern democratic institutions and, formation of a new political culture on the basis of the Constitution adopted in 1995.

The Constitution paved the way for economic and political reforms. The new national legislative acts enable real democratic institutions, where rights and freedoms of the citizens are guaranteed. It is remarkable that all this could happen under very difficult conditions when the country had to overcome the post-Soviet inertia syndrome and effects of the Asian financial crisis.

The Presidential form of government helped the country to successfully come out of the post-Soviet economic and political chaos. Political stability made the Kazakh economy attractive to foreign investors. The infrastructure was being improved and agriculture got a boost. New employment opportunities also emerged, and a strata of "middle class" was also being formed.

The third stage of development began in 2001. In this stage, a socio-economic breakthrough was achieved. Our country became a regional leader. Democratic traditions of the multi-ethnic and multi-religious society of Kazakhstan took firm roots. The following years were marked by an active national dialogue on the most effective ways of furthering democratic reforms. Principally, higher social goals made up the agenda of the day. New challenges and threats persistently demanded more dynamic modernization of the whole system of socio-economic and socio-political relations. "Democracy is not something to be declared, it has to be experienced", said Nazarbaev in an interview to the newspaper "Geneva Diplomatique". The democratic principles developed by the Western world do not in any way clash with the traditional values of the Kazakhs, even though in form and genesis the two are different. Democracy is not just a system, it is a culture by itself. One may talk about the success of democracy only when its humane character gets properly synthesized with the ethnohistorical culture of the people. The standards of democracy are common but in different countries they acquire different shades. This does not mean that today's Kazakhstan should adjust itself to European standards.

In Kazakhstan the democratic principles are being consistently inducted into the state and social life by forming a legitimate state and a suitable political system. By properly comprehending the processes of democratization of society, we can formulate further reforms and initiate a wide-ranging social dialogue on issues such as: increasing the role of political parties, improvement of election legislation, local self-government, increasing role of non-governmental organizations, civil society, strengthening of freedom of the press, and introduction of private land ownership.

Recent events demonstrate that the international situation is becoming more and more complex and contradictory. New risks and threats origins are emerging which cannot be explained with our usual perceptions. But one thing is clear: problems of the modern world are multi-national in character which means that united efforts are required to solve them.

NOTES AND REFERENCES

1. Address of the President of the Republic of Kazakhstan N.A. Nazarbaev "Novy Kazakhstan v novom mire"//http://www.mfa.kz/rus
2. Konstitutsiya respubliki Kazakhstan. – Almaty, 2006. – p. 7. – (Art, 46).
3. Kazakhstan v izmenyayushchemsya mire. Vystuplenie Ministra inostrannykh del RK Tazhina M.M. v Vashingtone, 8 May 2007 / /http://www.Acorda.kz/ru
4. Nazarbaev N.A. Epitsentr mira. – Astana: Elorda, 2001. – p. 12.
5. Shaumyan T.L. Indiya – budushchee ekonomicheskoe chudo Azii / / Indiya i mir. – M, 2000. – p. 34.
6. Ashok Mukherjee. Ekonomicheskie i gumanitarnie svazi RK smirovym soobshchestvom // Diplomaticheskii kurer. – 2007. – No.3. – p. 54.
7. Nazarbaev N.A. Kazakhstan osushchestvlyaet strategicheskoe dvizhenie k demokratii // RIA Novosti. – 2007. – 15 July.

6

Revived and Invented Traditions in the Political Systems of Central Asian States

A.A. Galiev

The word 'tradition' by itself implies some sort of continuity. However, some constructivists believe that even tradition can be invented.[1] The invention of tradition may have the same purpose as turning history into mythology, i.e. mythification of history. This is not accidental.

Both history and invented tradition are, two sides of the same coin. Mythification of history as a 'word' is an attempt to legitimize the present and prepare a base by going back to one's past. On the other hand, invented tradition is an action, a ritual that illustrates the myth as a 'word'.

Tradition can be invented as well revived. In practice, however, not all traditions get revived because different models are applied in the formation of a state. Some ready-made models may not always serve the interests of those who may be involved in the formation of a State. That is why elements from different models are amalgamated. Thus, while the political systems of the states of Central Asia are based on Western models, different traditional institutions have also been revived and installed within their political systems. These revived traditional institutions along with mythification of history serve as archetypes, which have been in existence from the very beginning. This provide a sort of legitimacy to the State.

This article is an attempt to explore the traditional institutions of Central Asia and show their role in present-day politics.

KAZAKHSTAN

Council of Aksakals (Elders): A revival of Council of Elders is taking place in almost all regions of Kazakhstan. Such councils exist within the administration (*Akims*) at various levels. These are social organizations having a multi-ethnic composition. They are consultative, though in some cases the decisions of *Aksakals* are given due attention. At the time of disturbances in Novy Uzen, the Council played a positive role in easing tensions.

Court of Biis: This institution has existed in the steppes for a long time and has been guided by the norms of traditional law, the "Zheti Zhargy" Code. It played an important role in the life of the Kazakh Khanate. Its role was somewhat belittled by the Tsar Administration though it was not altogether abolished. Presently, the *Courts of Biis* are being revived and in many districts of Kazakhstan such Courts have already been set up.

The Zhuzs: For Kazakhstan the problem of *Zhuzs* is one of tribalism. It manifests itself in the form of strengthening on the position of one's tribe (*Zhuz*).

The present economic condition of Kazakhstan has also contributed to the revival of tribalism which is more acutely seen among the rural population Young Kazakhs are migrating to cities in large numbers where they face a number of problems – lack of good command over Russian language, lack of education and bad living conditions. Unfamiliar living conditions lead them to group up with their own people, one's own tribe or ethnic group where they find some support. Sociologists have noted that marginalized people tend to adhere to traditions.[2]

In Kazakhstan, tribalism is continuously encouraged by organizing various jubilees of heroes of bygone days. The overt purpose is to strengthen Kazakh self-consciousness; but they are aimed at strengthening the latent ambitions of some leaders of the *Zhuzs*. Thus, the year 1995 was marked by the celebration of the Jubilee of Abai; and, in 1996 the Jubilee of Jambul was celebrated. Many Kazakhstanis considered these celebrations as a competition between the Senior and Middle-level *Zhuzs*. This is not too far from being true because the celebration of jubilees has become a sort of ritual feasts to serve establish traditional social relations.[3]

Some analysts believe that the main purpose of shifting the capital of Kazakhstan was "to widen the territory of settlement of the *Senior Zhuzs* that would weaken the influence of *Middle-level Zhuzs* in their original homeland".[4] It must be mentioned that in multi-ethnic Kazakhstan, Kazakh tribalism is no more an internal matter. Many ethnic groups of Kazakhstan, thanks to kinship, territorial and other relations with the original ethnos, consider themselves as part of some clan. According to A. Kurtov, the Russian-speaking population of Kazakhstan is against the elites of the *Senior Zhuzs*.[5]

The Khan Rule

The Kazakh Khans were one of the branches of the dynasty of Chingiz Khan. For a very long time the ideology of Chingiz Khan and a sort of "Chingizism' was prevalent in territories conquered by the Mongols which included Russia as well.[6] The basic idea of Chingizism was that only a descendent of the 'Golden Horde' of Chingiz Khan could become the legitimate ruler of the conquered territory. The Khanate was abolished in the 19th century when Kazakhstan became a part of Russia. Attempts were made to revive the Khanate during nation-freedom uprisings. The proposal to revive the Khanate came from Rahat Aliev who happened to be the son-in-law of the President of Kazakhstan.[7] Even he made an appeal in the name of past traditions, it was quite clear that lineage to become a Monarch is not enough.

The Cossacks

The Cossacks (sometimes spelt as *Kazak* as distinct from *Kazakh*) have several links with the Kazakh people. Presently, we are more concerned with 'Kazakness', the feeling of being a Kazak. The Kazakhs as well the Cossacks have the same origin. The idea of Kazkness has existed in the steppes of Eurasia since long and it is connected with shifting from one class to another. Traditionally, those people who ran away from the Uzbek Khanate were called as Cossacks (Kazakhs) and they were divided into squadrons of Cossaks (*Zhuzs*). The same name, Cossack (Kazak), was also given to Ukrainian and Polish peasants who ran away from their landlords in the fifteenth century.

Some other Turkic terms were also used in the sense of Kazakness: *Ataman, Koshevoi, Jigitovka*. Later, the Cossacks were crushed, and they became faithful defenders of an autocracy which they were opposing earlier. The government put more and more of these Cossacks on the borders of the empire to capture new territories and to expande 'Kazakness' as well. For example, on 10 April 1789, a large number of Bashkirs were included among the Cossacks. Almost the entire Kalmyk people were also turned into Cossacks. As the Empire moved further South and East, the Buryts, Ossetinians and Yakuts came to be included amongst the Cossacks.

The 'Cossacks' is very much diversified in terms of race as well as religion: racially they are Europoids and Mongoloids; and their religions are Orthodox Slav, Lamaism, Buddhism and Islam. Thus, 'Kazakness' (the Cossacks) is not an ethnos as such. It is an institution that was turned into a military-feudal group by the Tsars.

Kazakhness as the index of a separate group was disbanded after the October Revolution. It re-emerged, when on 26 April 1991 the RSFSR passed the Act on "Rehabilitation of repressed Peoples" which, mentioned the Cossacks. Afterwards some other acts concerning the Cossacks were also passed. All these acts encouraged revival of the Kazak movement in Kazakhstan. In Kazakhstan, unlike Russia, the Kazaks are considered not as an ethnic group but a martial race under the laws of another country. There emerged an inevitable conflict between the State and the Kazak people.

Mashrapas and Mohallas: The Uighurs of Kazakhstan live mainly in Semireche. They migrated from China in 1871. Their compact dwellings are organized around *Mohallas.* Every *Mohalla* has a chief called *Jigit-Bishi.* The inhabitants of every *Mohalla* help each other not only in difficulties but also during any socially significant activity. For this purpose, they have set up a Fund. Besides, the Uighurs have one more traditional institution called *Mashrap* which is a remnant of the old "Male House". In the early 1920s, it was banned by the Bolsheviks because it was competing with Party organizations. Now it has also been revived. Presently, it is banned in China.

Political Symbols: National state symbols and ideals are an inseparable part of formation and fixation of identity of any nation and State as a socio-cultural and political community. People create and revere their national and state symbols. Various flags, banners, seals attributes of self-identification and other form a significant part of these symbols.[8] The emergence and revival of statehood in Kazakhstan is also seen in national state symbols. The blue colour of the national flag Kazakhstan is, a reflection of ancient Turkish genealogical legends which relate the origin of Turks to the celestial sphere.[9]

The State symbols of Kazakhstan, have similarity with the emblem of the Kazakh Soviet Socialist Republic. This coincidence may be taken to be a link between modern Kazakhstan and its predecessor. In fact, almost all the former Soviet Republics have used Soviet State symbols in one way or the other; the Belarus Republic has even revived them completely. However, in the State Emblem of Kazakhstan all the Soviet elements have been discarded in favour of ancient symbols. *Shanyrak,* according to archaeologist E.E. Kuzmina and linguist V.A. Livshits, has its origin in the Indo-Iranian dwelling *Angarak* 'circle' (the circle of the sky).[10] The ears of wheat depicted in the emblem of the Kazakh SSR have been replaced by winged horses in the emblem of the Republic of Kazakhstan. These winged horses belong to the Sakas of the Issyk Kurgan region.

One of the political symbols of independent Kazakhstan is the *Alash Khan*. Apart from being a holy name for the Kazakh people it is also a self-designation. There is another aspect attached to this name; it served as the symbol of independence, during their history. It has played this role on a number of occasions, first during the time of revolutionary upheavals in Russia and USSR in the beginning and end of the 20th century when political parties and movements came into being and used the name, of this mythical progenitor of Kazakhs. The name Alash was used as a war-cry and helped unite the forces of three *Zhuzs.*

As far as Christian Orthodox is concerned, its followers have increased significantly. The Orthodox Church has launched a campaign for a climate of spiritual harmony.

KYRGYZSTAN

In the spring of 1989, the Kyrgyz national movement started to grow very fast. Problems of housing forced the Kyrgyz youth to symbolically occupy lands and construct houses in the occupied plots. They set up an organization called *Ashar*[11] which has played an important role in the formation of multi-party system in

Kyrgyzstan. In 1990, *Ashar* along with the *Asab* and *Atuulduk Demilge* (Peoples Initiative) formed the core of the movement called the Democratic Movement of Kyrgyzstan which spread all over the country.[12]

The Clan System: In Kyrgyzstan clan-tribal relations have always been very strong. For centuries, Kyrgyz society has existed as a confederation of several tribes divided into two major groups which are broadly known as the Southern and Northern Clans. During the Soviet period, these two groups worked as rivals in order to grab important posts in the Communist Party and the Government of Kirgiziya, as Kyrgyzstan was known then. The political balance that was maintained for twenty-four years by the First Secretary of the Communist Party of Kirgiziya T. Usubaliev (1961-1985) who had a very long political career. This was disturbed in 1985. After the resignation of Usubaliev in October 1985, A. Masaliev came to power. While Usubaliev represented the Northern Clan, Masaliev represented the Southern Clan. However, the political situation in the country did not change much.[13] The Northern Clans were urbanized, Russified and less dependent on religious traditions. The Southern tribes mostly represented agrarian regions which historically fell within the sphere of Uzbek influence.[14]

After suppressing the August 1985 putsch, President Akaev strongly established himself and took measures which proved that he understands the role of traditional-political structures. It is worth mentioning that Akaev proposed to give official status to *Aksakals*, the traditional heads of *Ails* (villages). They were to be paid salaries from the state exchequer.

In modern Kyrgyz politics, representatives of the old aristocratic *Manap* groups have started playing an important role. It is also worth mentioning that, when in 1991 Akaev was given the symbolic title of "Supreme Khan of Kyrgyz people", it helped in stabilizing his rule after the August putsch.[15] It is to be noted that, unlike Manap Rule, the Rule of Khans is not traditional in Kyrgyzstan.

The Court of Biis: In several regions of Kyrgyzstan, the courts of *Biis* and *Akskals* are being revived. A large range of issues falls within their competence. The Government has given due recognition to them.[16]

Political Symbols: Economically, Kyrgyzstan is one of the poorest countries of the world. But public dissatisfaction is partly neutralized by referring to the glorious past. While referring to its ancient history, the term "The Great Kyrgyz Power" is used. Huge sums have been allocated to celebrate the Millennium of the Kyrgyz Epic *Manas* and the Third Millennium of Osh city.

UZBEKISTAN

Mohalla and *Gap*: The *Mohalla* (neighbourhood community) as a form of organization of social life of a locality has been in existence since ancient times in Uzbekistan. It united many types of people irrespective of their social or ethnic background.

The Soviet union considered *Mohalla* as a remnant of the past. However, the *Mohalla* turned out to be very vital and the Soviet rulers decided to use it for their own interests. Activities of the *Mohalla* committees were also well-defined.

After independence the *Mohalla* are being revived as a democratic organ in self-rule. They have got official status as one of the important links of the State are covered in the Resolution on "*Mohalla* Committees in Cities, Settlements and *Kishlaks* of Uzbekistan".[17]

Thereafter, new tasks for the leadership of the *Mohallas* was created. The *Mohalla* is headed by a Committee that is elected in the General Body meeting of representatives of the majority of houses. The Committee elects a Chairperson from amongst its members. The Chairperson of a *Mohalla* Committee is known as the *Akskal* while his Deputy is called as *Muovin;* and, the Secretary is called *Kotib*. The *Mohalla* Committee also includes advisors who are elected from amongst elderly male persons having experience of organizational work. Separate Sub-Committees are formed for various activities like Welfare Sub-Committee, Sub-Committee of Ceremonies, Women's Welfare Sub-Committee, Youth Welfare Sub-Committee, War-Veterans and Labour Welfare Sub-Committee, Social Order Sub-Committee, Residence Maintenance Fund Sub-Committee and Finance Sub-Committee. There is also a Women's Council and a Community Court. In order to make the Chairperson and Secretary of the *Mohallas* more active and for support, the President of Uzbekistan on 23 April 1998 issued the Decree on "Support to Self-Rule Organs of Citizens". The salaries of the Chairperson and Secretary have been raised; Chairpersons have been allowed to receive full pension, wherever permitted.

Mohalla is the regulator of social and personal life in its territory. Traditionally, one main activity of the *Mohalla* Committees and Sub-Committees is organization of social activities. The residents organize *Hashar* (voluntary labour) every year from time to time.

The Uzbeks have the *Gap, Gashtak, Tukma* and *Ziofat* which are like the *Mashraps* of Uighurs. Most of the *Gaps* are unified communities with their own traditions. Members of each *Gap* help each other in daily life, take active part in preparations for marriage and extend help whenever needed. In *Gaps*, the main role is played by the mother-in-law or some other aged lady.[18]

Political Symbols: The formation of modern Uzbek nation proves the ideas of constructivists. A.Ilkhamov writes: "It would be naïve to assume the formation of Uzbek nation as 'an objective', natural-historical process. In fact, the process of formation of the modern Uzbek identity should be examined, in the formation of Uzbek SSR and be considered a result of a combination of the efforts of the ruling and cultural elites."[19] In view of the fact that modern Uzbeks combine in themselves various groups of Turkic and Iranian origin, it required great efforts to establish the antiquity of the ethnos. Amir Timur was selected as the great ancestor of Uzbeks. "The memory of Amir Timur has great significance for establishing a legitimate democratic State which could occupy its rightful place in the world community and for realization of the idea of Uzbekistan – a country with great future". This is what is said in school text books.[20]

To honour Amir Timur various localities have been named after him, monuments constructed and museums of Timur set up. The blue stripe in the flag of Uzbekistan, it seems, is meant to honour the memory of the flag of Amir Timur.[21] The national currency of Uzbekistan – Sum – also depicts the picture of Amir Timur.

TAJIKISTAN

Tajiks are the only Iranian-speaking people of Central Asia. Their traditional institutions are connected with agriculture and they are, in many respects, similar to the institutions of Uighurs and Uzbeks. The Tajiks have a community of seniors called *Mashvarat* which has neighbours as members. They have also got a Council of male members called *Jamomad*. There is a patrilineal clan group called *Avlod*.[22] *Avlod* brought under itself several generations of male relatives. It had a common household set-up and was the real owner of land. The formation of armed detachments of the Government and United Tajik Opposition took place on the basis of *Avlods*. The war became more fierce because of the revived spirit of 'blood for blood'.[23]

Clans

In Tajikistan, the division of clans has gone through several stages. First of all, it can be traced along the Northern line (roughly, Leninabad Region with a largely urban population) and the Southern agricultural region. The Leninabad group (Khujand clan) is traditionally one of the most powerful groups. During the Soviet period these people occupied key positions in the Communist Party as well as the Government. This trend has partly continued in the post-Soviet period too. For example, the former President of Tajikistan, R. Nabiev belonged to the Khujand clan. The Kulyab group, in contrast to the 'elite' North, represents the interests of the inhabitants of agricultural regions. When their representative E. Rahmonov came to power, key positions in Government, earlier occupied by Leninabadis were gradually taken over by the Kulyab group. The position of the Hissar community is somewhere midway between Leninabad and Kulyab, geographically as well as politically. The Gamar (Karategin) group has concentrated its interests around trade. They have provided the base for formation of the Islamic Revival Party and the extremist groups of militants – the Wahhabis. The positions of Pamirians (Badakhshan Group) is somewhat peculiar. They speak East Iranian languages and are mostly Shias while most of the Tajiks are Sunnis.[24]

Political Symbols

Tajiks consider themselves as one of the most ancient peoples of the world. The State emphasizes its continuity with early medieval states, primarily with the rule of the Samanids who had their capital in Bukhara. In 1999 the 1100th Anniversary of the Samanid State was celebrated in Tajikistan. The name of Shah Ismoil Somoni who was a patron of science and arts is greatly revered in Tajikistan. The highest mountain peak of Tajikistan has been named after him (it was earlier known as Peak of Communism).[25] The national currency of Tajikistan is also called Somoni.

The crown is a very important state symbol of Tajikistan which is not accidental. Folk etymology relates the ethnonym Tajik with the root *taj* meaning 'crown'.

TURKMENISTAN

Council of Elders

In the beginning of the 1990s Turkmenbashi started annual meetings with *Yashulylar Maslahaty* (Council of Elders). This organ did not have any legal authority. Very soon these annual meetings were turned into *Khalk Maslahaty* (Peoples Council) and the Council of Elders became just a part of "All Turkmen Conference". In 1992 when President Saparmurat Niyazov came out victorious in the General Elections, he took oath in the first Session of *Khalk Maslahaty*. Gradually, *Khalk Maslahaty* (Peoples Council) got more rights. *Khalk Maslahaty* was vested with maximum rights and powers after the attempt on the life of Niyazov in November 2002. After that incident, Turkmenbashi handed over all matters related to Presidential elections to *Khalk Maslahaty*. The main role given by its creator to *Khalk Maslahaty* was to maintain the existing political regime and preserve the socio-political system created by Turkmenbashi. According to observers, adoption of a new Constitution of Turkmenistan and abolition of *Khalk Maslahaty* will be a very important step in reforming the state system and bring it closer to international practice.[26]

Clans

In Turkmenistan, there are 9 (according to some other data, 14) tribes and more than 5000 small communities or groups. Amongst them the most influential are Tekins who gave support to the regime of Niyazov. After Niyazov assumed power, the Tekins came to occupy most of the important posts in the Government.[27] Dominance of Tekins has continued even after the death of Niyazov in December 2006. G. Berdymuhammedov who was elected President after the death of Niyazov is also a Tekin. According to the Internet publication "Khronika Turkmenistana", Tekins are occupying 75% of the highest posts in Government.[28]

It needs to be added that a touch of traditionalism is being given to new political institutions in Central Asia. For instance, the heads of administration are being designated as *Akim, Hakim, Rais*, etc. For the administrative-units also, traditional names – *Vilayat, Etrap* – are being used.

This article proves that traditional systems, though they are remnant of the past erstwhile era, continue to play a strong role in the countries of Central Asia.

NOTES AND REFERENCES

1. The invention of Tradition/ Eds Hobsbawm E, Ranger T. Cambridge, 1993, p. 320.
2. Osipova O. Amerikanskaya sotsiologiya o traditsiyakh v stranakh Vostoka. M., 1985. pp. 39-40.
3. Arutyunov S.A. Vvedenie/ Etnografiya pitaniya narodov stran zarubezhnoi Azii. M., 1981. p. 3.
4. Masanov N. Kazakhskaya politicheskaya i intellektualnaya elita: klanovaya prinadlezhnost i vnutrietnicheskoe sopernichestvo // Vesnik Evrazii. 1996. No. 2.
5. Kurtov A. Politicheskaya elita Kazakhstana. M. 1994. p. 5.
6. For details see Yudin V.P. Ordy: Belaya, Sinyaya, Seraya, Zolotaya+/ /Kazakhstan, Srednyaya i Tsentralnaya Aziya v XVI-XVIII vv. Alma-Ata, Nauka. pp. 106-164.
7. Aliev R. Respublikostan ili Kazakhskii Sultanat. Kakoi vybor my sdelaem? // Karavan. 2006, 1 September, 35 (851).
8. Gaziev K.S. Politicheskay nauka. M., 1994. pp. 341-342.
9. Zuev Yu.A. Drevnetyurkskie genealogicheskie predaniya kak istochnik po rannei istorii tyurkov. Summary of Ph.D. Thesis on History. Alma-Ata, 1967. p. 14.
10. See Akishev A.K. Put k zemle giperboreev // Iran-name. 2007, 1. p. 23.
11. "*Ashar*" is a traditional institution of mutual help in Central Asia.
12. Koichumanova Ch.U. Stanovlenie politicheskoi sistemy suverennogo Kygyzstana. Bishkek. 2004. pp. 67-68.
13. Abazov R. Politicheskie preobrazovaniya v Kyrgyzstane i evolyutsiya prezidentskoi sistemy //www.ca-c/org/journal/cfc-02-1999/st-06_abazov.shtml
14. Khanin V. Kyrgyzstan: etnicheskii plyuralizm i politicheskie konflikty//www.ca-c/org/journal/cfc-09-2000/18.khanin. shtml
15. Khanin V. Kyrgyzstan: etnicheskii plyuralizm i politicheskie konflikty//www.ca-c/org/journal/cfc-09-2000/18.khanin. shtml

16. Sud akskalov v Kirgizii //Nezavisimaya gazeta. 1996. 30 January.
17. Polozhenie "O mahallinskikh (kvartalnykh) komitetakh v gorodakh, poselkakh i kishlakakh respubliki Uzbekistan". Tashkent, 1993.
18. Arifkhanova Z. Traditsionnie soobshchestva v sovremennom Uzbekistane //www.ca-c/org/journal/cac10-2000/06.arith. shtml
19. Ilkhamov A. Formirovanie sovremennoi uzbekskoi identichnosti / Etnicheskii atlas Uzbekistana. Institut "Otkrytoe obshchestvo" – Fond Sodeistviya – Uzbekistan. 2000. p. 288.
20. Istoriya Uzbekistana. Period natsionalnoi nezavisimosti. Uchebnik dlya uchashchikhsya 11 klassov obshcheobrazovatelnykh shkol. Tashkent. 2002. p. 166.
21. *Op. cit.*
22. Obshchestvo i kultura Tajikistana. //countries/ topics/1/10/76 htm.
23. Shustov A. Tsentralnaya Aziya: renessans traditsionnykh institutov // www.fondşk.ru / articles. Php?id=1355
24. Kradin N.N. Elementy traditsionnoi vlasti v postsovetskoi politicheskoi kulture: antropologicheski podkhod // www.tazar.kg/ news.php?i=187
25. Obshchestvo i kultura Tajikistana // countries/ topics/1/10/76 htm.
26. Narodny Sovet Turkmenistana primet novuyu redaktsiyu konstitutsii strany// RIA Novosti. 26/09/2008
27. Kadyrov Sh.Kh. Turkmenistan: institut prezidentstva v klanovom postkolonialnom obshchestve// Vestnik Evrazii. 2001. 2. pp. 5-32.
28. Shustov A. Tsentralnaya Aziya: renessans traditsionnykh institutov // www.fondsk.ru / articles. Php?id=1355

7

Traditional Legal Institutions of the Nomads of Eurasia: History and Modernity

G.A. Urozbaeva

INTRODUCTION

The depth, scale, tempo and success of democratic reforms in countries which are in the process of transition from a totalitarian heritage to democratic systems depends upon the extent to their political and legal cultures. This is true of the young Central Asian states in their path to progress and democracy.

Traditional legal institutions and historically developed norms of Common Law were an inseparable part of the culture of the nomads of Eurasia. Development of democratic norms and a revival of national culture, language and traditions are taking place simultaneously in Kazakhstan.

The existing judicial system does not fully meet requirements of contemporary reality. For example, at the International Legal Conference (Prague, 17-19 May 2006), the ineffectiveness of the judicial systems was pointed out. A way out of the difficult situation could be alternate decisions through negotiations on controversial issues by partially reviving the "law of Natural Procedure" and creation of institutions of mediation for deciding civil and family controversies.[1] These elements existed in the legal systems of the nomads of Eurasia.

In the last decade of the twentieth century some scholars had expressed the desire to revive and adjust some of the traditional legal institutions, such as the court of *bii*s and *zargo* into the modern legal system. The well known legal expert of Kazakhstan, M. Narikbaev advocated revival of the court of *bii*s. But compatibility of the 'revived traditions' and modern reality is questionable. There is no doubt that some of the positive features of the court of *bii*s like objectivity, authenticity, openness and quick decision making on accumulated cases, could easily be adopted as effective instruments in modern judicial practice. However, the election of *bii*s and complicated modern judicial procedures might become a stumbling block in this regard. Perhaps, this was the reason that in the international conference on "The Kazakh Court of *bii*s – a Unique Legal System" (held in May 2008), the question of its revival was not even discussed.

Interest in the study of the legal systems of nomadic societies (sociums) is also explained due to the fact that it could throw to light some of the early history of law of in nomadic societies that of people with a settled agricultural civilization. The German scholar, K. Alinge says that "nomadic law with its primitiveness looks like a tiny hut in comparison with the grand building of Roman jurisprudence. But the foundation from which these two judicial systems grew was the same. The ideas of crime and its punishment, protection of property and inheritance are common to both systems. A description of these ideas of the law of the steppes could be just a small stone in the building of the history of universal law."[2]

Modern legal systems of Kazakhstan and the tribe are more or less integrated into the world legal system; at the same time, they form an independent 'Eurasian' group within the Roman-German legal system. The legal system of contemporary the Kalmykiya is part of the Russian judicial-legal system although the Constitution of the Kalmykiya that was adopted in 1994 is called "The Steppe Code". This name by itself signifies the historical connection of the Kalmykiya with the Jungar Khanate and the Code of Ikh Tsaaz of the year 1640.

The legal systems of the Kalmyks and the Kazakhs had several common elements due to special characteristics of the nomads. Presence of these common features has prompted some scholars to look for analogies in the traditional legal systems of the Kazakhs and the Kalmyks to the extent that it is being said that the Code of Tauke Khan, the old legal document of the Kazakhs, is simply a compilation of Kalmyk laws of Ikh Tsaaz. This totally unfounded because no historical-comparative analysis of these documents has been done. The reasons behind their emergence, their functioning and evolution and their special characteristics have not been taken into consideration.

The present article examines the traditional legal institutions of the Kazakhs like the Court of the *Bii*s in Kazakh society, the Court of *Zargo* in Kalmykiya, procedures of compromise and mutual consent which include fines (*kun* and *andz*). The sources of our study were the legislative documents of the Kazakhs and the Kalmyks, the Code of Tauke Khan, some general legal norms documented by Russian researchers of the 19th century, "Twelve Steppe Laws", "Ikh Tsazz" and "Khalkha Jirum".

In Soviet historiography, the history of nomadic societies was studied to understand their formation. The common laws of nomadic societies were studied by ethnographers and jurists whose task was simply to collect and describe these legislative norms.

But no schools were formed that could have helped in bringing out the characteristics and evolution of the common law in nomadic societies. After the disintegration of USSR, some scholars have tried to fill this gap and place nomadic societies in the universal-historical process. There being no properly developed school of thought for the study of nomadic societies, many researchers have adopted a nationalistic approach to mythologise certain phenomena and exaggerate their role and significance. But the regularities inherent in their legal systems, have remained outside the scope of such 'research'.

A special feature of the common law of the Kazakhs and Kalmyks is that any harm that has been caused by the guilty should be compensated in the form of property. Under conditions of a nomadic economy and the absence of corrective institutions, a unique system of legal norms was created to ensure the observance of law in the steppes. These legal norms were based on a unique scale of fines which were called *devyatok, pyatok, kun* and *andza*. The common features of the legal codes of the Kazakhs and the Kalmyks, the Code of Tauke Khan and the Code of Ikh Tsaaz, respectively, prompt us to look for common historical roots in them.

A characteristic feature of the legal system of nomadic societies was the procedure of compromise and mutual consent for solving controversial issues connected with infringement of property laws, crime against individuals, and matters pertaining to family and marriage. Looking at the process of judicial proceedings, we notice that they have certain common features such as: absence of judicial formalism (a court which is open, fast and without unnecessary bureaucratic delays), institution of reconciliation or mediation in the settlement of disputes; the concept of compensation for harm caused by a crime as a form of punishment. This approach to justice is very pragmatic. It is compensatory punishment, and not a punitive-educative action. This type of approach requires an effective mediation process between the victim and the offender. In the legal systems of nomad societies, primary importance has been given to the interests of the victim of a crime and, the criminal process was conducted, primarily, to restore the violated rights of the victim.

Mediation as a part of judicial process is a voluntary and confidential form of reconciliation of the sufferer with the suspected person (the accused) for which a neutral mediator is appointed. It has the potential and features to qualify as an independent legal institution. Mediation between two adversaries is one of the forms of restorative justice. The procedures of reconciliation and mediation are historically developed institutions. They have existed in the Mongol Empire of Chingis Khan and his successors, as well as Mongol, Kalmyk and Kazakh nomad societies during the 16th-18th centuries. The compromise and mutual consent procedures of common law as given in "The Eighteen Steppe Laws", "Ikh Tsaaz" and in Kazakh law have been discussed in several articles in which various kinds of punishment for crime against individuals have also been dealt with.

Russian officials and military officers in their documents pertaining to the common law of the Kazakhs have given a number of instances of practical restoration of usurped rights. According to the information given by Russian researchers, when pronouncing punishments for crimes against individuals, the time, place and peculiarity of crime were taken into consideration. P. Makovetskii writes: "The Kyrgyz people state that, in olden times, the murderer who had been secretly waiting for the most appropriate time to realize his intention to kill somebody was given death sentence, his *aul* (village) was plundered and his relatives were asked to pay a *kun* (fine) for the murder of an ordinary Kyrgyz equal to fifty camels."[3] A study of the life and decisions of the *bii*s shows that, for ordinary crimes, triple and double punishment were not given; on the other hand, there is a proverb that denies possibility of two punishments: "*Bir koidan eki teri soimaidy*" is 'you can't get two skins from one sheep'. There were cases when the court of *bii*s enhanced, even doubled the penalty; but they never combined together two different types of penalties. Therefore, it would not be incorrect to say that in olden times *kun*, death sentence and plundering of *aul* were never given as punishment in combination.[4] *Kun* as system of redemption could have variations. It depended upon the region, race and social class of the criminal and the victim. That is why the notes of Russian researchers mention different amounts of *kun*, varying from 100 to 7000 sheep. It is quite possible that Tauke Khan had only established the minimum and maximum amounts of *kun* and, within these limits the exact amount of punishment was left to the discretion of the court. In judicial practice instances of the *kun* of 1000 sheep for an ordinary person or 7000 sheep for the Sultan or Khoja are not available.[5]

It has been noted by D'Andre that "punishment for every crime, irrespective of its nature, was decided upon and served more by the discretion of the *bii* rather than on the basis of some legalities."[6] The *kun* was to be paid by all the co-kinsmen of the person committing the crime irrespective of their status. In the opinion of A.A. Slovokhotov, "the purpose of such a heavy fine was to deter everybody from indulging in the murder of any one else.[7] In the absence of a police apparatus and a unified centralized rule, the institution of *kun* in the Kazakh nomadic society served as the most effective instrument for maintaining law and order. The *kun* as a system of redemption was a measure of punishment for crime and, it was one of the ways of a compromise solution. S. Bronevskii has remarked that "the prosecution sides want that the murderer be handed over to them for execution; but they are pacified by the soft-spoken *bii*s who make the prosecution side agreeable to accept a certain amount of *kun* and a lavish party in lieu of the punishment."[8]

In Mongol and Kalmyk societies, there existed a unique system of fines in the form of *andza*. The Ikh Tsaaz Code clearly says: "If somebody kills a man, then, as per the Great Code, take from him one thousand sheep."[9] Possibly, the equivalent of one thousand sheep was three hundred thirty *andza*. The laws of Khalkha Jirum also say that of *andza* is a system of redemption for the crime against an individual.[10] Along with payment fine for the murder, Khalkha Jirum also mentions corporal punishment. Determination of these types of punishment was influenced by Manchurian and Chinese laws. Thus, for example, Article 2 of the Code for the year 1709 says:

> If someone commits a murder out of revenge or mischief, then he should be asked to pay a fine of thirty *berke* and three hundred *andza*. A murdered officer should be compensated by another man and a camel; and a non-officer should be compensated for by another man. If a man is not available, then a young camel and a five-year old horse should be given as compensation. The guilty person should be given hundred lashings of whip and made slave of the slaves in *hoshun*. If he does not have enough cattle for paying the fine of *andza*, then his head should be handed over to the wife and children of murdered person.[11]

The procedure of compromise and mutual consent of the common law as given in the "Eighteen Steppe Laws" can be seen in sections those places punishments for causing injury. For instance, injuries caused to the most important organs of the human body invite very strict punishment:

> If someone breaks another person's hand and the victim yet remains capable of working, then the guilty should be fined three *devyatok*. If the victim becomes incapable of work, the guilty person should pay *andza* for the murder.[12]

Articlc 89 of the Ikh Tsaaz says: "If someone cuts off any one of the six organs and parts of the body (eye, hand, leg) of another person, then he should be asked to pay five *devyatok* along with something valuable." In the laws of 'Khalkha Jirum', corporal punishment, arrest and confinement in a pit were added as forms of punishment. "Smashing both the eyes of person is equivalent to murder of the man. If someone smashes one eye, he should be fined fifty *andza* and whip an equal number of lashings." "If someone breaks another person's hand or leg but the victim later on if capable to work, the guilty should be fined three *devyatok*; if the victim remains incapable of work, the fine to be paid by the guilty person should be the same as for smashing an eye."[13]

According to Kazakh law, on serious injuries caused to the body leading to loss of work ability invite the fine of a full *kun* which could be equal to 1000 sheep, a camel and a carpet.[14] Such a heavy fine could compensate for the loss of the bread-winner of a family.

In Kazakh, Mongol and Kalmyk laws the most common type of fine was the *devyatok* which had existed in the empire of Chingis Khan. The purpose of these punishments was not only to give the victim a compensation but also, to desist deter offers from repeating such a crime in the future. Due to similarity culture, these three societies have some common categories of law pertaining to family and marriage, law of inheritance, collective responsibility, punishment, and legal procedures. Some differences have crept in due to external influences, geographical location and the influence of religion. For example, one of the characteristic features of the Kazakh and Kalmyk laws is the detailed procedure for executing a judicial verdict.

A look at the legislative documents of the 16th-17th centuries shows that, in the Mongol society of that period, there existed an established system of legal procedures. There were special persons called *elchi* whose duty was to bring the accused persons to the court, the accused could be detained for nine days for investigation and interrogation, searches could be carried out and evidence of witnesses admitted before passing a verdict. The Law of Six Khotuns says:

> In order to catch fugitives who have gone to some other *khoshun*, one *elchi* each from every *khoshun* should be sent. If some *khoshun* does not send the *elchi*, take two horses from that *khoshun*." Article 88 of the Great Law of the Year of Monkey and Article 33 of the laws of Ikh Tsaaz also emphsize the significance of *elchi*: "The accused should be sent with an *elchi*. If the accused is sent without an *elchi*, the case cannot be settled." "If someone kills an *elchi*, he should be fined a *devyatok*.[15]

In case the guilt of the criminal has been established, then there was a set procedure of investigation: "If the accused does not admit his fault twice, he should be asked to give three sheep. If even after this he does not admit his fault, the Khan should be asked for further advice. The Khan sends the *elchi* to take one horse. If obstacles are created at this stage, the horse along with the harness should be taken. If the accused still does not admit his fault, then four horses should be taken by sending one *elchi* each from the four *khoshuns*. If the accused does not admit his fault even after this, then eight horses should be taken by sending eight *elchis*. If the accused still does not admit his fault, then the following action should be taken. Take the cattle by increasing the number of *elchis*." Similarly for finding evidence of theft or other crimes, all classes of the population were subjected to search, irrespective of their status and ethnicity. "If *noion, tabunang* or someone else enjoying power refuses to be searched, then, after clarifying the reason for such a refusal, take *andza* from him. Take one horse from the person who does not come for search. The person carrying out search takes a *devyatok*."[16]

There are also differences in the mechanisms of executing judicial verdicts. We see that the documents of the Mongol and Kalmyk law are silent about this aspect, i.e. execution of judicial verdicts. The later Code of 1709 says in Article 9:

> As soon the thief has been convicted, the *elchi* should give him 80 lashes before the *noions* and *saits* who have pronounced the judgment; after this the thief should be made to take 100 rounds of the monastery (*khure*) and bow 1000 times before the statue of Buddha. The *noion* should appoint an observer and the thief should fulfill all this within ten days. If the executors show any prejudice, they should be deprived of their bread.[17]

In Kazakh law, one of the ways of executing a decision was *barymta* (raid and driving away the cattle). "This was an organized raid of the *aul* of the defendant which was carried out as per the verdict of the court of *bii*s or of the senior person in case the accused refuses to satisfy the demands of the plaintiff."[18] For such a *barymta*, special conditions were laid down: firstly, departure for raid was to be done only in daytime; secondly, the *barymta* raid was declared openly with the aim of undoing the harm be it theft, kidnapping of a bride or murder."[19] With the permission of the elders the plaintiff had the right to carry out *barymta* with his co-kinsmen. After returning from the *aul* of the defendant, the plaintiff had to inform the *akskal* or the *bii* about the quantity of the cattle captured which should not exceed the quantity of the cattle lost by him. If the *barymta* was carried out incorrectly, then a penalty was imposed.

Thus, we see that the laws of the Kazakhs and the Mongols of 16th-19th centuries are not simply a copy or an imitation of laws that were existing earlier. They are a result of law-making activities over a long period of time. Some similarities regarding imposition of fines in the Code of Tauke Khan and the Ikh Tsaaz do not prove that the compilers of the Code of these laws had copied them fully; the similarity was due to similarities in nomadic way of life.

Proper study, analysis and revival of any of the traditional legal institutions requires a careful approach before embracing a new and modern legal system. It is only after this, that some of the elements of the traditional legal system may be applied in a modern legal system. One such elements is mediation which could become an effective mechanism in violation of laws related to property.

NOTES AND REFERENCES

1. Materialy Mezhdunarodnoi sudebnoi konferentsii. – Prague, May 2006. .//uppc.perm.ru/_res/main docs/389.doc.
2. Alinge C.. Mongolische Gesetze. Darstellung des geschriebenen mongolischen Rechts.(Privatrecht, Strafrecht u.Prozeß). - Leipzig, 1934.-P. 158.
3. Makovetskii P.E. Materialy dlya izucheniya yuridicheskikh obychaev kirgizov – Vyp. 1. Materialnoe pravo. – Omsk, 1886. – p. 46.
4. *Ibid.*, p. 64.
5. Kulteleev T.M. Ugolovnoe obychnoe pravo kazakhov. (S momenta prisoedineniya Kazakhstana k Rossii do ustanovleniya Sovetskoi vlasti). – Alma-Ata: Izd-vo ANKazSSR, 1955. – p. 84.
6. Delo o komandirovanii v Kazakhskuyu step chinovnika po osobym porucheniyam D'Andre // TsGA RK. F.4. – Op. 1. D. 401. – L. 99-104; Chernovie zapiski chinovnika osobykh poruchenii komissii D'Andre ob obychayakh kazakhskovo naroda // TsGA RK. F. 4. – Op. 1. D. 2380. – L. 55.
7. Slovokhotov A.A. Narodny sud obychnovo prava kirgiz Maloi Ordy // Trudy Orenburgskoi uchenoi arkhivnoi komissii. – Vyp. 15. – Orenburg, 1905. – p. 63.
8. Bronevskii S. Zapiski o kurgiz-kaisakakh Srednei Ordy // Otechestvennie zapiski – Ch. 42 – Kn. 120. – pp. 75-88.
9. Ikh Tsaaz ("The Great Code"). Pamyatnik mongolskovo feodalnovo prava XVII v. Transliteratsiya svodnovo oiratskovo teksta, perevod, vvedenie i kommentarii S.D.Dylykova. – M.: Nauka, 1981. – p. 14.
10. Khalkha Jirum. Pamyatnik mongolskovo feodalnovo prava XVII v. Svodnii tekst i perevod Ts.Zh.Zhamtsarano. Podgotovka teksta k izd., redaktsiya per., vved. i primech. S.D.Dylykova. – M.: Glavnaya redaktsiya vostochnoi literatury, 1965. – p. 114.
11 *Ibid.*, pp. 69-70.
12. Pamyatnik mongolskovo feodalnovo prava XVI-XVII vv. Mong. tekst, transliteratsiya mongolskovo teksta/ Per. s mongolskovo, kommentarii i issled. A.D.Nasilova. – St.Pb.: Peterburgskoe vostokovedenie, 2002. – pp. 16-25.
13. Ikh Tsaaz ("Velikoe Ulozhenie")... P.21; Khalkha Jirum. Pamyatnik mongolskovo feodalnovo prava XVIII v... P.70.
14. Delo o komandirovanii v Kazakhskuyu step chinovnika po osobym porucheniyam D'Andre ... L. 58.

15. Pamyatnik mongolskovo feodalnovo prava XVI-XVII vv... p. 42; Ikh Tsaaz ... p. 17.
16. Pamyatnik mongolskovo feodalnovo prava XVI-XVII vv... p. 48.
17. Khalkha Jirum. ... p. 29.
18. Levshin A.I. Opisanie kirgiz-kazachikh ili kirgiz-kaisatskikh ord i stepei. Ch. 3. – Etnograficheskie izvestiya. St.Pb., 1832. – p. 85.
19. Grodekov N.G. Kirgizy i kara-kirgizy Syrdarinskoi oblasti. – T.1, Yuridicheskii byt. – Tashkent, 1889, pp. 170-171.

8

Democratization in Central Asia and the US Experience

Kukeyeva Fatima

Central Asian views their relations with the United States are diverse, reflecting the multi-dimensional character of international relations and the variety of issues that concern both the US Administration and governments in the region. Today, the new risks and challenges to national, regional, and international security include: international terrorism, proliferation of weapons of mass destruction, national and ethnic conflicts, illegal drugs traffic and organized crime. Another issue to be added to this list, is the democratic development or "democratization" which unites internal and foreign political issues regarding the stable development of countries.

The United States policy has attached great importance to the democracy and the development of civil society in the region. American analysts and policymakers repeatedly emphasize that poor political and economic transformation is a threat to the prosperity and the freedom of nations in the region and the security of Central Asia as a whole. The Talbots Doctrine declared that democracy and a market economy form the main factors of political stability and national economic prosperity.

In the Freedom Support Act (1992), the US Congress, considered the new geopolitical situation after the disintegration of the USSR and sought to prevent the spread of religious extremism in the interest of national security.

In 1997, Assistant Secretary of State, Strobe Talbot emphasized the inter-relation between successful democratic reforms and stability both inside, and outside the region. He identified assistance to the development of democracy as a priority of US policy in Central Asia.

In the international agreement for the "Silk-Way Strategy" (1999), Central Asia, the United States and the European Union have stressed the importance of human rights and democracy.

During her visit to Kazakhstan in 2000, Secretary of State Madeleine Allbright placed a special emphasis on democracy. The current Secretary of State Condolizza Rice has also stressed the importance of democracy in her visits to Central Asia in the Fall of 2005.

The events of September 11, 2001 have made promotion of democracy one of the major geopolitical goals of US Central Asian policy. In 2002 the Bush's administration adopted two principal policy initiatives. First, through the Freedom Act in Afghanistan the US intended to establish democracy and promote civil society as a means of eradicating terrorism. Second, the 2002 'US National Security Strategy' pledged the use of military, political and economic resources to promote open societies and the development of democracy in defense of US national interests.

However, if the Kazakhstan and Kirghizstan researchers on the whole recognize the need for American support to promote democracy, they do criticise the methods used by the United States government to achieve this purpose. Tajik and Turkmen analysts in particular doubt the validity of Western-style democratic values in Central Asia.

In analyzing US policy in the region before the events of September 11, 2001, Kazakhstan experts came to the conclusion that the degree of democratization and the reformulation of the political system as well as the process of forming civil society did not achieve the degree of success expected by the West. The Kazakhstan analysis met some coolness and disappointment in USA.

To explain the "insufficient promotion of democratic reforms", the Central Asian authors list a number of factors.

- The US Americans takes a short-term view in supporting the establishment of real democracy. In the article, "Problems and Calls for Democratization in Central Asia", L. Bondarets of the International Institute of Strategic Research under the President of the Kyrghiz Republic emphasizes: "Our opponents for some reason overlook that they consistently built [their own] democracies over long historical period" (Problemy i Vyzovy Demokratizatsii v Tsentralnoi Azii, Bondarets L.M. Politika, Politicheskaya Nauka, Bishkek, 2005).

- The absence of democratic institutions of authority, and the lack of experience with private ownership in the post-Soviet period complicate the creation of a lawful state, market economic relations, and civil society. These states follow a pattern of "democratization from above" where authorities do not involve the citizens, or, at best, limit access to the process of political transformation.
- Furthermore, the presence of weak oppositions which have no clear strategy results in their political failure, preventing the constructive participation of political opponents in the evolving democratic processes. Coordination both between and within opposition groups is weak. In most countries the opposition also has a weak financial base.
- The absence of a real opposition encourages the State authority to try in every possible way to neutralise any potential opposition such as by co-opting potential rivals in State posts, creating so-called 'pocket' opposition groups or, in rare cases compelling certain persons to emigrate.

Though recognizing the US role in democratisation of Central Asian countries, Kazakhstan political scientists point out contradictions in American policy. In particular, they question a foreign policy line in which Washington pursues economic cooperation and military bases by dealing with authoritarian leaders instead of pushing these governments towards democratic political reform. Taking into account the fact that representatives of the old Soviet and party elite [nomenclatura] retained power. Washington has concentrated more on dealing with people in power than on creating new institutions of management.

For example, despite the appeals of human rights organizations to consider Uzbekistan as a country "causing special anxiety concerning religious and other freedom", the United States did not hide its intentions to establish long-term relations and cooperation with high interest in the development of oil and gas deposits in Uzbekistan. After the events of September 11, 2001 and the beginning of an American military presence in Central Asia, discussions about a "new Washington strategy in the region" have started. Assistance to democratic development acquired a new thrust with the re-definition Central-Asian countries as being in the "first line of combating terrorism". Programmes of the US State Department provided direct support for independent mass media, development of political parties, religious freedoms, administrative reforms, education and health care financing.

Traditional announcements about the United States interests in political stability, democratization and economic prosperity in Central Asia are linked with American strategic interests in the region. It is necessary to include the existence of authoritarian regimes in this policy, which means "to lead two incompatible things to consensus. (Tsentralnaya Aziya do i posle 11 Sentyabrya: Geopolitika i Bezopasnost, Almaty, 2005).

Due to Washington's shifting priorities, Kazakhstan analysts developed doubts about the motives of US foreign policy. One thesis argues that the United States asserts "responsibility for security and stability in the region using democratic rhetoric and economic control levers as the means of pressuring ruling elites with the goal of creating a net of political regimes which are effectively controlled by Washington" (N. Omarov. Sostoyanie i Perspektivy Mezhgosudarstvennovo Sotrudnichestva, Kyrgyzstana i SShA v 90-e gody XX - Nachale XXI vv. // Politicheskaya sistema SShA i Voprosy Demokratizatsii v Stranakh Tsentralnoi Azii, Almaty, 2005, SS.93). Murat Laumulin, a well known political scientist in Kazakhstan, also considers that Washington formally proclaims democratization and human rights "as principles of American foreign policy, but in reality … [they are] often used as methods of political influence and tools of pressure" (M. Laumulin. Politika SShA po Podderzhke Demokratii v Tsentralnoi Azii, Politicheskaya Sistema SShA i voprosy Demokratizatsii v Stranakh Tsentralnoi Azii, Almaty, 2005, SS 31-33).

Before the removal of the American base from Uzbekistan and the events at Andijon the American policy on democracy and human rights issues suffered from serious contradictions. Today, the US Department is a vocal critic Karimov's internal policies.

While relations with Tajikistan are focused on combating terrorism and the drug, so pressure is being applied going with the assistance of social organizations to liberalize the mass media.

In spite of the criticism by American investigators of the Turkmenbashy regime, there are practically no announcements by the State Department concerning the human rights situation in Turkmenistan.

Such policy is interpreted in Central Asian states as duplicitous. Official Washington continues to assert that it is doing its best to support the democratization process in these states. At the same time, the United States began to determine its relations depending on their readiness to provide USA with military bases and access. The question of further political and social reforms to strengthen democracy in the region appears to be of low priority. Therefore, Central Asian leaders have the right to ignore US appeals for democratic reforms and continue their policies in whatever direction they find necessary.

As the Kyrgyz political scientist, N. Omarov remarks, it will be difficult for the United States to support the process of democratization if "regional partners are the corrupt and despotic regimes which live in fear of their own population" (N. Omarov, Metodologicheskie Aspekty Samoidentifikatsii Gosudarstv Tsentralnoi Azii v globalnom prostranstve, SShA i strany Tsentralnoi Azii: Realii i Perspektivy Vzaimootnoshenii, Almaty, 2004).

Proponents for "special models of democracy" stress that democracy exists in different variations. And raises one basic question: Who will guide this democracy?

As R. Abdullo, the political scientist from Tajikistan, argues: "The rejection of totalitarianism does not at all mean the direct arrival of western-style democracy" (R. Abdullo, Strany TsA i SShA: Evolyutsya Vzaimootnoshenii // Tsentralnaya Aziya i Kavkaz, 2005, No. SS. 47-57). Researchers like Abdullo argue for the role of authoritarian governments to provide a smooth transition from the legacy of Soviet totalitarianism to a democracy.

In a more anti-US vein, other researchers show their aversion to Western values in the struggle against international terrorism advocated by the current Bush administration. They see it as a rigid imposition of alien social values and political cultures on the Muslim people. From this point of view, the US approach to democratization of society in the Central-Asian states shows a lack of desire to recognize and take account of the unique features of developments in the region.

In response to Western criticism of the authoritarian government in Tajikistan and other Central Asian countries, Abdullo opposes the 'absolute' idea of democracy, something that must be the same everywhere, with his own idea that democracy is of great value. It should be adapted to different circumstances in different times and places. He argues that "for Tajikistan now the main value is Tajik statehood. To achieve statehood today requires a democratic form of management which is characterized by a dominant presidential authority with all the features of political life that follow from it to serve the country well" (R. Abdullo. Strany TsA i SShA: Evolyutsya Vzaimootnoshenii, Tsentralnaya Aziya i Kavkaz, 2005, No. SS. 47-57).

Concerning the Andijon events these authors believe that the US position is irrational because it gave a call for an international investigation which could increase the conflict between local factions.

These analysts believe that the slow rate of democratizing internal and external policy has encouraged the growth of social movements like so-called "Colour Revolutions". These have shaken the political system in some countries while creating a sense of concern in others.

Kyrgyz and Kazakh political scientists characterize the Spring 2005 events in Kyrgyzstan as a "revolution", a "coup d'etat" or the replacement of authority. It is necessary to recall that Kyrgyzstan under the President A. Akaev once had the reputation of being the most democratic republic in Central Asia. The Kyrgyz political elite positioned itself as supporters of democracy. Post-Soviet Kyrgyzstan has followed the ways of social and economic modernization, of free-market institutions and a creation of conditions for democratic society. But such impediments to development like tribalism, despotism and corruption continue.

Central Asian political elites should draw their own conclusions from the events in Kyrgyzstan. Kazakhstan has set itself high standards for economic development but now faces the objective necessity to improve its standards of political development. US assistance can only speed up this process, but only up to a point.

After the Kyrgyzstan, Central Asian experts have tried to understand the reasons behind the "Colour Revolutions". The policy of external pressure for speeding up democratic reforms is one of the versions discussed in scientific circles. But opinions are divided between those who consider "revolutions" as a result of external influence by non-regional players, especially the US, and those who suggest searching for the real internal reasons.

Experts who support the first opinion believe in the impossibility of effectively integrating Central Asia as a significant geopolitical region in the global international system along Western line. They argue that the Central Asian elite has no other strategy than to promote the authority of its clan. Therefore, US pressure forms the base for revolutions through such as a critique of authoritarian regimes, charges of violating Human Rights and corruption and the political use of financial, economic, technical, or humanitarian assistance. Here, NGOs and opposition groups and public relations programmes apply pressure to promote a positive US image (Khalil Kh. Gosudarstvennaya Politika SShA v Tsentralnoi Azii na Sovremennom etape, Sayasat 2003, No.11. S. 11).

On the other hand, analysts who suggest causes of the 'revolutions' in internal political and economic processes, mention the following factors: legitimacy crises of existing regimes; serious contradictions inside the ruling elite; active opposition and its populist slogans; lack of authority to use force; and unresolved problems between the advanced north and the underdeveloped south of the country. Events in Kyrgyzsthan and Uzbekistan give evidence for the presence of both internal and external causes.

First, Kazakh and Kyrgh political scientists believe that the present political crisis in Uzbekistan and the change of government in Kyrgyzstan are not a continuation of the democratic and peaceful revolutions in Ukraine and Georgia. The struggle between the northern and southern clans for authority, low living standards and social differentiation are the discrepancies in political consciousness in society. However, the situation in Kyrgyzstan only imitates events in Ukraine and Georgia. As to the Andijon events, Central Asian analysts recognize that deep social problems that have existed for a long time in the impoverished population.

Second, analysts continue to discuss Islamic component in the Kyrghiz and Uzbek events. Some similarly equate the problem of Islamic and secular components because in Islamic countries (Uzbekistan, Tajikistan) any anti-governmental movement should be Islamic by definition. However, the initial version presented by the mass media that the events in Andijon were completely prepared by Islamic extremists has not proved to be true.

Third, some researchers consider that the regime change in Bishkek and events in Andijon are the result of the drug mafia. Undoubtedly, the problem of drug-trafficking and the "shadow economy", have an influence on the region as a whole. However, it would be a mistake to conclude that events are shaped only by drug business interests.

There are three factors. First, the internal factor. Revolutionary explosions created a loss of popular confidence in the governments of the countries along with absence of a real democracy and the low living standards.

Second, the post-Soviet elites have been poorly prepared for transformation, by and large.

Third, the independence of the Central-Asian states and their integration into the world community is occurring under the conditions of globalization.

Fourth, the geopolitical characteristics of the region generate problems: especially the closed transport space with limited outputs to world markets and the under-developed network of communications. These include irregular distribution of water and other natural resources, of the population, and numerous zones of ecological disaster. There are enormous empty territories and inhospitable living conditions in Kazakhstan and Turkmenistan.

These contradictions amplify complex social and economic conditions, cause an aggravation of tensions among political, ethnic, religious groups and clans struggling for power and, encourage extremist and terrorist organizations, especially the Islamic fundamentalists.

Finally, non-regional actors also play a role. The success of the Georgian and Ukrainian opposition has strengthened Washington to promote democratization throughout the post-Soviet space. In March 2005, President Bush declared his intention to actively assist the "Colour Revolutions" and to support a rapid action Special Corps to support new democracies. This declaration has created ambiguous reactions in countries of Central Asia.

9

Political Transformations in Kazakhstan

M. Sh. Gubaidullina

INTRODUCTION

Political reforms in Kazakhstan are part of a continuing process of issues related to political and economic modernization. These are still being discussed because there is the need to develop a balanced political system in which civil society as represented by political parties, unions and organizations would occupy their proper place.

Our basic premise is that, due to changing dynamics in the country, it is not possible to state unequivocally about a balanced political system. In fact, civil society as its most important component carries hardly any weightage; the State and the President as its executive Head are extremely strong.

In the systemic relations there is unequal dependence on internal and external factors; it is applicable to the choice of political course too. The State is interested in stability of the socio-political system while it is carrying out institutional reorganization.

GENERAL CHARACTERISTICS OF THE POLITICAL PROCESS

Political developments in Kazakhstan have led to the creation of "democratic" model of the political regime which is typical of many of post-Soviet countries. Certain steps in the direction of democracy are being taken even though they are still far off from creation of a real democracy. The foundations of a market economy and liberal legal-social relations are being laid.

At the same time, Kazakhstan has its own specificities about political modernization and the conditions for carrying out reforms.

These specificities include: Soviet type of inbred mentality, tribalism and clan spirit, competence of those participating in the political processes and the political situation as seen in the correlation of forces established during the 18-year period of President Nazarbaev.

FACTORS OF INFLUENCE

The most significant and foremost *internal* factor influencing the political process is the economic factor: the tempo of growth or recession. Here, we include the political will of authorities which should be capable of supporting a stable political situation. We also consider the involvement of civil society in the political process. The basic form of democracy which was mentioned at the time of independence of Kazakhstan seems like a distant dream.

The present system is such that it reacts to a situation. It is subject to political vacillations. The typical way of overcoming problems is more or less standardized in the form of declarations and strategically defined national programmes with ambitious aims.[1]

The political dimensions of transformation processes has a significant influence on the internal ones too. On the one hand, the international legal obligations of Kazakhstan for creating a democratic and legitimate State are being addressed and, on the other hand, the State is responsible for its foreign policy initiatives which require adequate internal political reforms.

The relations of Kazakhstan with OSCE are noteworthy because OSCE expects Kazakhstan to go take further in political and legal reforms. Relations with European Union are also developing in the same direction. The Commissioner of the European Commission on External Relations and European Neighbourhood Policy, Benita Ferrero-Waldner has advised Kazakhstan "to continue the path of genuine democratic reforms" for which it can "approach the European States which have got wide experience of framing the constitutional laws."[2]

In the context of the recommendations of the European Commission, the Government of Kazakhstan passed four new Bills in November 2008, which provide for a multi-party system in Parliament. Minister of Foreign Affairs, M. Tazhin said Kazakhstan has demonstrated its "consistency in the realization of national priorities for developing Kazakhstan into a modern competitive State, taking into consideration of its own international experience as well the international standards."[3]

METHOD

Relations between internal and external political factors which influence the political process and modernization in Kazakhstan can be analyzed through traditional approaches. In this connection, the theory of public choice is very important. Empirical material and several types of comparative studies provide a picture of the process of political decisions while behaviourist approaches explain the results of the policy by looking at special features of the existing political system.

Let us examine some of the realities reflecting the political processes in Kazakhstan and its political line.

Discussions of the current political process can be started with two documents: the Declaration "On Sovereignty" and the Constitutional Act "On State Independence of the Republic of Kazakhstan".[4]

While the Declaration talks about "creating a humane democratic legitimate State", the Act affirms "the right of the Kazakh nation to self-determination" and "the resolve to create a civil society and a legitimate State". The first one puts emphasis on "democracy" and the second on "civil society".

In a recent official document it is stated that by 2005 Kazakhstan has created more than 5000 NGOs. Also, "significant results have been achieved so far as Human Rights and freedoms, freedom of speech, freedom of organization and freedom of political expression are concerned". Moreover the Ombudsman's role in Human Rights has been widened.[5]

It must be mentioned that the contents of any political process are determined by the problems faced by the society and country at a particular time. Looking at the society which found itself engulfed in disintegration of the USSR and engaged in building up an independent Kazakhstan, one notices the tendency of gradual withdrawal of society from participating in this process. The sovereignty of Kazakhstan in the internal life of the country is determined, by actions of the State in its own name. The Government is responsible for "deciding on its own all the questions related to political, economic, social and national-cultural construction in the RK, and its administrative-territorial structure". (Declaration..., para 6)

The process of political development in Kazakhstan is that in the monocentric regime of today, the ruling elite is getting aloof from society; and, the quality of governance hardly matches with the range of acute problems that are being faced by the people.

Social interests have practically remained outside the scope of economic results and political processes in spite of the fact that, from the very beginning, society has been involved in these processes indirectly, if not directly. We would like to agree with the views of the political analyst and sociologist Sabit Żhusupov who says that, "The tempo and degree of political reforms in Kazakhstan are determined more by the State organs of power than by the needs of the society and challenges faced by the country."[6]

The basic contradiction is that citizens' initiatives, mainly supported from outside, do not find adequate support and popular acceptance in the Kazakh society because they are not participating actively in the reform process. Speaking figuratively, it has got almost 'frozen' while waiting for real reforms in the political system.

"Independence" and "national sovereignty" have become key words in the political vocabulary of the ruling elite. They are being used very often in various kinds of State symbols and political rituals. For the first time, expressions like "national sovereignty" and "national approach" have acquired a special meaning in the building up of the State and political system.

The term "National interest" has acquired high significance, particularly in systemic changes.

In political reconstruction, Kazakhstan has been able to avoid internal conflicts on nationalistic grounds and has maintained its multi-national and multi-faith character as a State. However, latent attempts of some nationalist-political groups to change the policy of the State and turn it into an ethnic-national State could lead to a state of conflict.

THE ECONOMY AND POLITICAL PROCESSES

Political development during a period of transformation has an ambivalent and contradictory feature: how to guarantee stability of the system while establishing democracy under pre-critical and critical economic conditions.

In the first half of 1990s, Kazakhstan gained rich political experience in dealing with a number of problems immediately after independence. President Nazarbaev stated that "successes in the economy of Kazakhstan have laid a reliable foundation for continuing with political modernization of the society and democracy. We have built our State on the principles of Western democracy while taking into consideration experiences of advanced East Asian countries and the specific nature of our multi-ethnic and multi-religious society."[7]

In the period of transformation, a proper connection between the economic reforms and the political process is needed. Here is an example which shows how the present system of strong Presidential power was established.

Establishment of the State and political institutions of Kazakhstan took place under difficult conditions that prevailed during the 1990s when the centrally controlled economy was being replaced by a market economy. The economic crisis was accompanied by political uncertainties. The Government and political institutions with their incomplete structure were not in a position to react effectively to the crisis. For example, while adopting a strict credit policy by reducing the expenditure on social programme the Government dragged society into a long-drawn social crisis. Even introduction of the national currency, Tenge could not stop a sharp increase in prices and inflation rate reached up to 43%. Because representative institutions in 1993 were hardly effective, there was a conflict between various political branches of the State structure leading twice to dissolution of the Parliament.

The first Parliament of sovereign Kazakhstan was almost non-functional because it was not able to carry out legislative reforms which were essential for implementing economic reforms. The Supreme Soviet of Kazakhstan remained dissolved during December 1993 to March 1994 and internal policies were being decided by the Executive – the Government and the President.

The first professional parliament of Kazakhstan elected on 7 March 1994 also turned out to be unprepared to face the economic crisis of the time. The newly elected Parliament also remained dissolved from March until December 1995; but this time the decision to dissolve Parliament was taken by the Constitution

Court. Continuous confrontation between the Executive and the Legislature was headed in a dangerous direction. The Head of the State strove to have a compact Parliament which could work harmoniously with the Executive. In both cases, the President took strong decisions and issued Ordinances. Ultimately, it became possible for the Legislature to restore its work.

However, the Executive itself got split due to mutual acrimonies. The President criticised the government strongly and asked the Government to accelerate the economic reforms. In this regard E. Ertysbaev said, "Just one month after the new Parliament began its work, Members proposed a no-confidence against the Government and Prime Minister S. Tereshchenko. President Nazarbaev was compelled to come to Parliament so that a dialogue could be established."[8] No constructive settlement between the Legislature and the Executive could be found. In the spring of 1994, the President reorganized the system of State power. The Office of the President of Kazakhstan and Cabinet Secretariat were formally separated.[9]

The Parliament, toeing the line of the President in its resolution of 27 May 1994, blamed the Government for the failures during the initial years of sovereign development. It is interesting to see how the Parliament has argued its position. It admitted that "wide-ranging reforms in social relations, State structure and economy were inevitable" at the same time it said that "while the Government adopted the path of market economy, it was, in fact, trying to block it which led to economic chaos. It said that the Government was to be blamed for this crisis because it "lacked a common national programme of reform". While criticizing the Government the Parliament did not comment on the actions of the President.

The Government was forced to prepare an Anti-Crisis Programme of Action and carry the reforms forward. But it was destined to resign. The Supreme Soviet expressed lack of confidence in the socio-economic and legal policies of the Government and called for formation of a new Government which should be able to implement the national programme of reforms. This was also a dramatic period for the Supreme Soviet as it was also dissolved in the spring of 1995.

The mechanism for division of power among different branches was not taken to its logical conclusion. The balance of power was not realistic; and, the status of the Supreme Soviet, President and Government with respect to one another was not fully clear. A little later the Constitution of 1995 laid the foundation for a system in which the President was given directive powers; and, the Government was given executive powers but without any authority.

An assessment of the political and economic processes taking place in the post-Soviet space has been given by G.K. Helbright who writes: "Transformation from communism to market economy is a process which requires time as well as proper thinking. There is still hope of a stable and strong Government, of gradual and careful actions and systematized rule of law."[10]

Administrative Reforms

Action was initiated for strengthening the institutions of power based on an administrative system of governance rather than on social structures.

In the present bureaucracy, there is division of labour and a hierarchy. Recruitment of staff is done on the basis of sound criteria. Most of the Government officers are not sufficiently competent, they lack initiative, and are afraid of responsibility. The V. Pareto Law that 80% of useful work in any office is performed by just 20% of the staff is true in Kazakhstan. It may also be added that Parkinson's Laws regarding professionalism in a bureaucracy are equally applicable to Kazakhstan: number of staff and volume of work are not at all connected with each other. The number of staff continues to grow irrespective of the increase or decrease of work.[11]

Kazakhstan needed administrative reforms for good governance. 'Good governance' means an active, effective and incorruptible State administration which goes by the rule of law and has respect for Human Rights. Good governance implies economic growth combined with political stability, political pluralism and accountability.

However, a new bureaucracy empowered with the authority of enforcement is getting entangled in politics. Further, administrative reforms are connected with "increasing the effectiveness and results of the work of the administrative machinery. That is, the officials should serve the people in a real sense".[12]

In order to set up an effective administration machinery in Kazakhstan to international standards and practices, a whole set of measures were taken up to improve the quality of State service and administration, to cut down the size of the bureaucracy and to increase the professional level of personal. The European Union and the Kazakh Agency of State Service Affairs has implemented the Programme of "Assistance of European Union for reforming the structure of State Service during 2006-07."[13]

POLITICAL REFORMS

Socio-economic reforms and political programme of the last few years have made reforms irreversible and accelerated the political transformation of the country. Plans for development of Kazakhstan up to the year 2010 as a part of a long-term strategy up to 2030 have given a wider dimension to political processes, and ensured that implementation would occur in a systematic manner. The National Commission for Democracy and Civil Society is working on the 'National Programme of Democratic Reforms for the Period 2006-2011'. In the autumn session of the Parliament (September 2005), the leadership approved this programme.

The aim of this programme is to form an effective political system which should be capable of meeting the interests of the country while creating a civil society. The purpose is to build a more balanced, flexible, effective democratic political system in Kazakhstan.[14]

In the opinion of the First Secretary of the Central Committee of the Citizens Party of Kazakhstan, A. Peruashev the political system of Kazakhstan has reached a stage which would mainly consist of modernization of all its elements.

POLITICAL PARTIES AND THE FURTHERING POLITICAL PROCESS

One of the conditions for successful modernization is that different parties should participate in the processes of political reforms. While a multi-party political system has been introduced in Kazakhstan, the political parties and organizations talked about liberal ideas and values. In the present set-up their activities are being regulated by the Constitution and the Acts[15] pertaining to social organizations and political parties.

Political parties of Kazakhstan, for the first time, got the right to participate in elections to the legislature – the 13th Supreme Soviet which was to be constituted in March 1994. As a result, the first professional Parliament of Kazakhstan was elected which functioned for almost one year (April 1994 to March 1995). Thereafter, elections to the new Parliament (December 1995, September 1999) were held with the active participation of candidates from different political parties. It was a foregone conclusion that the results of elections to the 3rd Parliament in September 2004 would also go in favour of the leading party of the country, the "Otan" party. In political circles, they were seen as a rehearsal for the Presidential elections of 2005.

The years, 2004-2006 can be termed as the years of preparation and organization of Parliamentary and Presidential elections. During this period, one could notice fierce activities at the political and party levels and a picture of apparent contradictions was emerging. External relations of Kazakhstan with OSCE, and conversely, of OSCE with respect to Kazakhstan, led to a fierce competition between the ruling and opposition parties.

It is worth noting that in spite of the minimum limit of membership being fixed at 50,000 members, there were about ten political parties in Kazakhstan in 2006. The parties are notionally divided into three groups: pro-President parties, opposition parties and others. The first group includes the "Otan" party (Leader N. Nazarbaev), the "Asar" party (D. Nazarbaeva) (they got merged the new "Nur Otan" party), Citizens Party consisting of members engaged in the mining business, and Agrarian Party consisting of members from leading food grains companies. The merger of "Otan" and "Asar" parties marked an important stage in the political system of Kazakhstan because it strengthened the executive power vertically and provided a unified political orientation to the Kazakh ruling class.

The group of opposition parties includes "Ak Zhol" (Leader A. Baimenov), "Real Ak Zhol" (former associates of A. Baimenov) and the Communist Party of Kazakhstan (S. Abdildin). Others include the "Auil" party, Party of the Patriots of Kazakhstan, Democratic Party of Kazakhstan and "Ruhaniyat". These parties can be termed as 'virtual' parties because their position is decided by their leaders.

The main weakness of the party system rises from the fact that, from the very beginning, several restrictions were imposed and it was not allowed to grow in an objective manner through party channels. The absence of a full-fledged party system in Kazakhstan is also connected with the fact that a Kazakh society is still not differentiated on the basis of political interests. Moreover, "during the 15 years of formation of the new political system there was no mechanism for the role of political parties in the power structure".[16]

Only the President's power is recognized as the regulatory authority. It was the President of Kazakhstan who initiated the process of political reforms. This situation was raised in many social discussion during the elections to Parliament in September 2004 and August 2007; and, during the Presidential elections of 2005.

GROWTH OF A STRONG PRESIDENTIAL RULE

The crisis period of the 1990s was marked by a three-fold division of power, strengthening of the Executive and building up of the powers of the President. While the Declaration of State Sovereignty of the Kazakh SSR of 1990 mentions a change in the status of the President, the 1991 Act "On State Independence of the Republic of Kazakhstan" defined the position of the President as Head of State and as Head of the Executive with regulatory powers. The Kazakhstan Constitution of 1993 has demarcated the executive power in a section which mentions precedence of the President before the Government. It also increased some responsibility of the Government.

Strong Presidential powers were required at the time when economically and politically Kazakhstan's economy was considered weak by outsiders as incapable and as a country governed by the outdated Constitution of Soviet times. The socio-economic and political situation was in a critical state.[17]

Thus, socio-economic crisis, political instability and an amorphous legislature led to the institution of Presidentship acquiring the foremost place in the power structure. President became an influential factor in the political system of Kazakhstan. The specific feature of the President's position is status as the guarantor of the stability of the State as a whole and the ruling political class.

Regarding his powers, the President emphasized the decisive role of the economy in influencing politics. The economy, has become one of the influential political factors in which "functioning of an authoritative political system during the modernization of a developing society is manifested in the implementation of an effective economic strategy which is also able to ensure national sovereignty".[18]

Kazakhstan has been living like a controlled democracy. In the social consciousness of the people, the idea has taken root that there is no other way but to except the President as Head of the power structure who is elected for a seven-year term. In his speeches, Nazarbaev always stresses that it is "the strong Presidential system of rule that has demonstrated its maximum suitability when foundations of a new political system and market economy are being laid. Historically and politically, that is the proper stage for transformation and modernization of the political system".[19]

Analysing the speeches of President N. Nazarbaev on political themes we can draw the following conclusion: the successes of the Kazakhstan model are linked to a strong Presidential system of rule and adoption of this form of rule.

Nazarbaev has been occupying the post of President since 1991. The status of the President was decided in the first Constitution of 1993; two years later the Constitution of 1995 extended the powers of the President till the year 2000.

The Constitutional status of the President of the Kazakhstan has three basic components: firstly, President is the Head of State; secondly, President is the guarantor of the Constitution and 'arbitrator' who ensures harmonious working of State organs; thirdly, he is the final executive authority.[20] Looking at the events of the last two years, we can say that the position of the President has become stronger.

The Presidential elections of 2005 was a turning-point in the liberalization of political processes through the participation of the opposition parties and reforms of the political system. However, the absence of a political culture and a competitive politics led to scandalous charges during the election campaign for the post of President in 2005.

The main points of criticism have been: absence of democracy, falsification of the election process and corruption. These charges came, most unexpectedly, from some representatives of the ruling class, former and existing politicians and opponents. It included persons, like A. Kazhegeldin (former Prime Minister), Z. Nurkadilov (former Mayor of Almaty and a member of Parliament), Tiyakbai (Speaker of the *Majilis* and one of the leaders of "Otan" party); also leaders of the democratic party "Ak Zhol".

Their speeches displayed the possibilities of conflict in the ruling class of Kazakhstan. However, these internal political differences did help to raise the level of political debate.

The position of other competitors to the post of President (Tuyakbai, Baimenov, Abylkasymov, Eleusizov) got blurred because it had been unanimously predicted that Nazarvaev would win the elections. Very soon they disappeared from the political scene because they got very few votes. E. Ertysbaev is of the opinion: "As the days of voting were approaching the Kazakhstani voters, who wanted to vote in favour of opposition candidates, finally reconciled with the inevitable defeat of their candidates; and, they simply ignored the elections." Foreign observers had a different opinion about these elections calling the "election situation in Kazakhstan as very dull and drab".[21]

The elections failed to achieve their main goal. The Kazakhstan opposition parties were not able to overcome their internal contradictions. Consequently, they got relegated to the periphery of political life.

After the Presidential elections of December 2005, the people of Kazakhstan were not clear about the country's wanted to know what was going to happen to the politics. Political groups within the power structure and around it had significantly lost their influence.

The State quickly responded by proposing a National Programme of Reforms. Nazarvaev's victory in the Presidential elections of 2005 gave him a *carte blanche*. In the first place, he chose economic modernization within limits.

TRANSITION FROM PRESIDENTIAL SYSTEM TO PRESIDENTIAL-PARLIAMENTARY SYSTEM

The discussions on political reforms in Kazakhstan acquired a real shape after 16 May 2007 when President Nazarbaev proposed to the Parliament some amendments to the Constitution. These were passed on 21 May.[22]

After the dissolution of the 3rd *Majlis* (20 June 2007), it was announced on 18 August 2007 that mid-term elections will be held on the basis of proportional representation. Political parties again became active.

The idea of a monopolist party was becoming dominant, and in the Parliamentary elections of 2007, unprecedented strengthening of the "Nur Otan" party was witnessed.

In the next stage of transformation of the political system although new opportunities were given to political parties, the small parties faced a very difficult situation because they had to cross the minimum barrier for their recognition. In any case, results of the elections to Parliament held on 18 August 2007 caught many people in Kazakhstan and outside unaware. Nobody thought that any party except "Nur Otan" could reach the highest legislative organ of the country.

The constitutional reforms proposed by the President in May had important changes regarding the term of the President: beginning from 2012, the term of the President would to be reduced from seven years to five years; and, one would be able to be elected as President for not more than two consecutive terms. The Parliament approved this Amendment but did not make it applicable to the First President of Kazakhstan. In this way, N. Nazarbaev "has legitimately become the life-long President of the country".[23]

In the opinion of I. Zvyagelskaya: "The very essence of the new model is that President as well as Parliament are trying to ensure a smooth transition from a Presidential Republic to Presidential-Parliamentary Republic. The President is in a hurry to lay the foundation of a new political system which would make the choice of the President predictable and there would be a clear-cut distribution of power between the authorities." A. Baimenov of "Ak Zhol" party is of opinion that a change-over to the proportional representation and increased role of *Majlis* in the political system is the key element of political reforms and the process of strengthening political parties has now started. I believe that these changes are going to be another step in the direction of building up of a stable political system with several strong parties."[24]

Amendments to the Constitution gave legitimacy to latter changes in the Constitution of 2007. A Presidential-Parliamentary type of republic was sought to be formed in which the authority of President would dominate even more and the single-party Parliament would be given wide powers, the single party in Parliament being the President's party "Otan". At least one thing was clear: the parliamentary system will not be able to function effectively in the absence of political pluralism through a multi-party system and active functioning of social organizations.

Very soon more changes were introduced. In November 2008 at a meeting of the Government under the Chairmanship of the Prime Minister Maksimov, four Bills on further democratization and liberalization were approved which included Acts "On Political Parties" and "On Changes Regarding Activities of Mass Media". Through these Acts, a mechanism is being created so that the *Majlis* of Parliament would consist of at least two political parties. In the new bill, the seven per cent barrier has been retained; however, if only one political party gets the requisite number of votes, then the next political party receiving the maximum number of votes is allowed to be accepted as a member of the *Majlis*.

The new bill has also fixed the accountability of the Government. The Prime Minister can be appointed by the President only after consultations with various groups within the Parliament and after obtaining the consent of a majority of members of the Lower House. As a consequence, the Parliament would get wider powers. But the President continues to be the main centre of power.

NOTES AND REFERENCES

1. Long-term of development of Kazakhstan up to the Year 2030// Inform-analit. Website of the Agency for Strategic Planning of the Republic of Kazakhstan: http://www.strategy.kz/debate_plan.html#7; Strategic Plan of the Development of the Republic of Kazakhstan up to the Year 2010// Inform-analit. Website of the Agency for Strategic Planning of the Republic of Kazakhstan: http://www.strategy.kz/debate_plan.html#7; Kazakhstan on the threshold of a new spurt in her development. Strategy for Inclusion of Kazakhstan Amongst 50 Most Competitive Countries of the World. Address of the President of the Republic of Kazakhstan N.Nazarbaev to the Peoples of Kazakhstan, 1 March 2006.// www.akorda.kz/page.php?page_id=32&lang=1&article_id=1426
2. Meeting of the Commissioner of European Union with the Chairman of the Senate of Parliament N.Abykaev. // Kazakhstan Today. 19 October 2006.

3. Kazakhstan has taken a very important step for modernization of its political system. //Kazakhstanskaya Pravda, 14 November 2008.
4. Declaration of State Sovereignty of Kazakh SSR. Alma-Ata, 25 October 1995. //MEA of RK: http://www.mfa.kz/rus/index.php?/base=28article_id=19; Constitutional Act of the Republic of Kazakhstan, 16 December 1991, [1] 1007-ÕII "On State Independence of the Republic of Kazakhstan" //Vedomosti Verkhovnogo Soveta. 1991, No. 151.
5. See Decree of the President of the Republic of Kazakhstan dated 29.11.2004, No. 1474 "On Further Strengthening of the System of Protection of Constitutional Rights and Freedoms of Peoples and Citizens" ? //www.zakon.kz/law/English/M542P10388.DOC
6. Zhusupov S. Tsentry prityazheniya //Ekspert. 08.11.2004 (www.expert.ru/printisues/expert/kazakhstan/
7. For a comparison of these poimts we can cite earlier as well as later documents: Declaration and the Constitutional Act (1990-1991), President's Addresses to the peoples of Kazakhstan of the years 2003, 2004, 2005. In all of these documents the vocabulary used is similar, and statements in favour of democracy and legitimate State are also identical (Website of the President of RK //www.akorda.kz/www_akorda_kz.nsf/sections).
8. Ertysbaev E.K. Demokratizatsiya v Kazakhstane: 1990-2000. – Almaty, 2000. p. 157.
9. Ordinance of the President of the RK "On Reorganization of the Office of the President of the RK and Cabinet Secretariat", dated 13.04.1994. As a separate institution of State power the Office of the President of the RK is engaged in improving the State structure and strengthening the staff which is evident in the regularly issued Ordinances "On the Strength of the Staff and Structure of the Office of the President of RK". Outdated Ordinances of the years 2000-2004 have been replaced by a new Ordinance, dated 11 February 2008, No. 533 //http://www.akorda.kz/www/www_akorda_kz.nsf/sections
10. Rethinking the Future. Views of leading American scholars on modern development // Mirovaya politika i mezhdunarodnie otnosheniya. 1998. No. 11. P. 19.
11. Parkinson S.N. Zakony Parkinsona /Translation from English. Minsk, 1997. p. 8.
12. Nazarbaev N.A. Kazakhstan na puti uskoryonnoi ekonomicheskoi, sotsialnoi i politicheskoi modernizatsii. Poslanie Prezidenta RK narodu Kazakhstana. 18 February 2005.
13. The Programme of the European Union consisting of two projects worked on improvement of professionalism of the State personnel of Kazakhstan, improvement of the system of basic and advanced training, and development of standards for functioning of the structure of State services //http://www.delkaz.ec.europa.eu.

14. Obshchenatsionalnaya programma modernizatsii kazakhstanskovo obshchestva ("Dorozhnaya karta") //http://www.apn.kz/?chapter_name=advert&data_id=354&do=view_single/ 27.04. 2006.
15. Act of the RK "On Social Organizations". 31.05.1996. [1]3-1; Act of the RK "On Political Parties". 15.07.2002.[1]344-2//http://www.pavlodar.com/zakon/?dok=00060&all=all
16. Junusova Zh. Parlamentskie fraktsii kak factor demokratizatsii politicheskoi sistemy: sravnitelny analiz //Sayasat 2008. No.4. P.23.
17. Nazarbaev N. Kazakhstan na puti uskorennoi ekonomicheskoi, sotsialnoi i politicheskoi modernizatsii. Address of the President of the RK to the Peoples of Kazakhstan. 18 February 2005. // www.akorda.kz
18. Khoros V.G., Cheshkov M.A. Politicheskaya modernoztsiya v posttraditsionnykh obshchestvakh //Avtoritarizm i demokratiya v razvivayushchikhsya stranakh. – M, Nauka, 1996. P.16.
19. Nazarbaev N. Kazakhstan na puti uskorennoi ekonomicheskoi, sotsialnoi i politicheskoi modernizatsii. ... 18 February 2005. // www.akorda.kz
20. Constitution of the Republic of Kazakhstan, dated 30 August 1995 (along with Amendments of 7 October 1998). Official edition. – Almaty, 1998. Art. 5, Sec. 1-2, Art. 23, Sec. 1)
21. Kazakhstan Today, 4 December 2005, and Kazakhstan Today, 5 December 2005.
22. A new stage of democratization of Kazakhstan - accelerated growth of a free democratic society. Speech of the President of the RK N.A.Nazarbaev at the Joint Session of the Houses of Parliament. 16 May 2007// http://www.akorda.kz/; Act of the RK dated 21 May 2007, No. 254 "On making Amendements to the Constitution of the RK" // Kazakhstanskaya pravda. 22 May 2007.
23. Kazakhstan Today. 19 May 2007.
24. Eksperty i politiki o konstitutsionnoi reforme v Kazakhstane // Ezhednevnaya obshchestvenno-politicheskaya respublikanskaya gazeta, No.213 (16361), 17.11.2007.

10

Constitutional Principles of the Republic of Kazakhstan and Transformations in Kazakh Politics

S.Zh. Sapanov

One of the main features of the constitutional development of independent Kazakhstan is the ongoing reforms of the political system. There are some peculiar characteristics in the process of transition to a democratic societies in Kazakhstan. It was able to avoid political crises which could have led to destabilization of the society. The most evident element in this regard is strengthening of the Presidential form of government rule which got the final legislative approval in 1995.

The idea of the Presidential system has been borrowed from foreign political and State institutions. To this day, this system is functional in more than 63 countries of the world. There are two models of the Presidential system – American and French. In Kazakhstan, as also in many other CIS countries, the French model was adopted.

At present, the structure of State organs of power in Kazakhstan is almost similar to the Fifth Republic of France in which the President has the status of Arbitrator; and, so, remains above other organs of power.

The 1958 Constitution of the French Republic actually gave a long-term and State structure which was acceptable to all. This Constitution came as a result of the influence of Gaullism on constitutional principles. Gaullism has three elements: independence, theory of participation and constitutional doctrine.[1]

It has been pointed out by K.I. Baizkova that the constitutional experience of France has significantly influenced and continues to influence, the constitutional development of many countries. The French Declaration of Human and Citizens' Rights of 1789 not only laid the foundation of the constitutional history of France; it also, determined the development of the institution of human rights in the whole world.

Unlike many other countries, France has had sixteen different Constitutions for more than 200 years. The Constitutional experience of the Fifth French Republic was determined to be closer to the needs of Kazakhstan. Of course, it would have to blended with experience the Kazakhstan.[2]

As per the traditional classification of political regimes, the French Republic is neither purely parliamentary nor purely Presidential. It is a combination of both the systems. During the period of the Fifth Republic the Constitution of 1958 has strengthened the democratic principles and introduced certain changes in decision-making.

France has highly developed and stable legal and political institutions. It is a country with long democratic traditions and effective mechanism of State organs through which continuity and stability of political regimes is maintained. France is a liberal democracy. In a very short period of time, it has evolved from a parliamentary regime to the regime of personal authority of a single person. The President of the French Republic has relegated other State organs – the National Assembly, the Senate and the Government to the background.

Article 5 of the Constitution says that, the President of France is the guarantor of national independence, integrity of its territories and observance of international treaties and agreements of the Union. He looks after the functioning of the Constitution. President of the country is the highest arbitrator for all the problems faced by the Government. He is politically not responsible for his actions and is not controlled by anybody.

Creation of the institution of President of Kazakhstan in 1990 was one of the basic steps in formation of Kazakh Statehood. There were several objective and subjective factors behind it.

Towards the end of 1980s, the Soviet Union was in a serious crisis. At that time Kazakhstan was gradually widening its sphere of competence and acquiring the components of sovereignty. At the same time, structural changes in political, economic and social spheres in Kazakhstan and intensification of international aspect in politics required the setting up of a new constitutional organ of power.

In the short period of its existence, the institution of the President of Kazakhstan has undergone significant evolution – from the imperfect and vague status of the President of Kazakh SSR to a well-defined system.

Adoption of the Constitution of 1995 in many respects changed the balance of political institutions with more powers being given to the President of Kazakhstan. While drafting the 1995 Constitution, the shortcomings of the Constitution of 1993 were kept in view and international legal aspects, including the French Constitution, were taken into consideration.

Soon after independence, President Nazarbaev said:

> We have to think about the whole situation carefully, analyze our development from the point of view of the experiences of other countries and compare where do our reforms and newly set up institutions stand in comparison to the best experiences of other countries.[3]

The prerogatives of the President with regard to Government have been drastically changed. He is authorized to appoint the Prime Minister of the country and accept his resignation. On the recommendation of the Prime Minister, the President appoints or replaces Ministers and State Secretaries. He chairs the meetings of the Government and exercises control over its work by signing Ordinances and Decrees passed by the Government.

As far as the foreign policy of the country is concerned, the President's traditional prerogatives are: representation of the country in its relations with foreign nations and international organizations; accreditation of ambassadors, declaration of war (with the permission of Parliament); ratification of international accords and agreements. These prerogatives have enhanced the powers of the President in matters of foreign policy.

The institution of President in Kazakhstan has its own history. The question of establishing a Presidentship in Kazakhstan came up as a result of the character of federal relations within USSR and creation of the post of President of USSR in March 1990. On 24 April 1990 at the XII Session of the Supreme Soviet of Kazakh SSR, the Act "On Instituting the Post of President of Kazakh SSR" was passed. On the same day, N.A. Nazarbaev was elected as the President of Kazakhstan.

There was a number of factors which led to the creation of the post of President. The most common factors are: weakening of executive power in USSR after the abolition of Articles 6 and 7 of the Constitution of USSR; and serious economic and social problems; attention to the problems of discipline and rule of law. Instituting the post of the President of Kazakhstan was looked upon as a chance to develop Statehood, to remove negative tendencies in the economic and social spheres and to ensure inter-ethnic harmony.

Initially the legal status of the President was determined by the Act of Kazakh SSR on "Instituting the Post of the President of Kazakh SSR and Amendments in the Constitution" of 24 April 1990. This Act envisaged general, equal and direct election of the President by a secret ballot for a term of five years.

The institution of the President in Kazakhstan further developed as a result of basic documents in which the independence of Kazakhstan was formulated: Resolution of the Supreme Soviet of Kazakh SSR on "Declaration of State Sovereignty of Kazakh Soviet Socialist Republic" dated 25 October 1990 and the Constitutional Act of the Republic on "State Sovereignty of the Republic of Kazakhstan" dated 16 December 1990.

In view of the fact that, in the first stage of development the institution of President had been implanted into the Soviet system of rule from outside, the constitutional status of President could not acquire the shape of a full-fledged and logically well-formed institution. That is why along with building up of the statehood of Kazakhstan the constitutional status of President also needed to be clarified after independence.

The Constitution of Kazakhstan was adopted by the Supreme Soviet on 28 January 1993. The institution regulated by Article 75 of Chapter 13 which states: "the President of the Republic of Kazakhstan is the Head of State and heads the unified system of executive power." The President was also the guarantor of observance of rights and freedoms of citizens of the country, the Constitution and laws of the Republic.

According to the 1993 Constitution, the formation of a Ministerial Cabinet and its activities were controlled by the Parliament but the Cabinet was answerable to the President. In that Constitution, no norms were laid about the rights of Parliament to initiate impeachment of the President; and about the right of the President to dissolve the parliament.

According to most political analysts of Kazakhstan, the following factors have led to a strong Presidential rule in Kazakhstan: low political culture, lack of developed political parties and mental make-up of Kazakh society which tends to prefer uniform thinking, traditionalism and patronage.

According to some Kazakhst scholars, the main negative feature of the 1993 Constitution was that it did not clearly decide the form of government. So, there were tensions in the political sphere due to the existence of two parallel centres of power – President and Presidential Administration on the one hand, and the Supreme Soviet on the other hand.

The Constitution of 1993 marks the beginning of a new stage in the evolution of statehood of Kazakhstan. The Constitution defined the concept of division of power and Presidential rule in clear and unequivocal terms; and formulated clearly the rights and freedoms of the citizens.

In March 1995, a Session of the Assembly of the peoples of Kazakhstan (APK) was held. This Assembly turned itself from an organ of representatives of all ethnic communities of Kazakhstan into a consultative-advisory body attached to the President. This Session in which social activists, leaders of political parties, scholars and journalists took part, passed a Resolution on conducting a referendum about extending the powers of President Nazarbaev up to 1 December 2000. The referendum was held on 29 April 1995 in which 91.3% voters took part; and, 95.4% votes were polled in favour of extending the powers of N. Nazarbaev to the 2000.

On 30 August 1995, a national referendum on acceptance of the new Constitution of the Republic of Kazakhstan was conducted in which 89.1% of the voters voted in favour of the new Constitution.

According to Article 44 of the Constitution of Kazakhstan, the President can examine a Bill passed by the Senate within a period of 15 days after which he either signs it or refers it back. For further discussion and voting. The President can also call the First Session of Parliament as per the powers vested in him under Article 44 of the Constitution and as per the Rules and Regulations of the Parliament of Kazakhstan. The President has the right to dissolve parliament under Article 63 of the Constitution. There are many countries in the world, including countries with parliamentary system (e.g., Italy and Germany) where President has been given the power to dissolve parliament.

Under the Constitution of 1993, the President of Kazakhstan and the members of Supreme Soviet, Cabinet Ministers, Judges of the Supreme Court and Supreme Arbitration Court had the right to initiate legislation. But under the Constitution of 1995, the President can make an appeal against legislative initiative. He has the authority to issue Ordinances under circumstances specified in the Constitution.

The President of Kazakhstan has the powers to decide basic principles of the internal and external policies of the country. Several Kazakh scholars justify the necessity of this norm because political parties in Kazakhstan have not been established; as such, they are not represented in Parliament in such numbers so as to express the will of their voters.

The main military rights of the President are: to function as the Supreme Commander of the Armed Forces; to appoint and dismiss highest military commanders; declare a state of war in case of military aggression; and, to announce full or partial mobilization of reserve forces. Questions of war and peace remain within the competence of Parliament.

In this way the Constitution adopted in 1995, envisages a strong Presidential rule. Some of its elements have been taken from the constitutions and established practices of other countries.

The institution of the President of Kazakhstan has undergone significant evolution thanks to so many political events that occurred in the initial years of the independence of Kazakhstan and formation of the model. Only citizens by birth can be candidates for the post of President of Kazakhstan. They should be not less than 40 years in age, should know the Kazakh language and they should be seconded by 2% of the voters.

In comparison, the requirements for the post of the President of France are quite democratic. The minimum age prescribed for the President of France is 23 years and the candidature has to be seconded by 500 persons holding elected State positions of France – Mayors, Members of Parliament and Members of Municipal Councils. The State bears all expenses of election campaigns and all candidates are given equal time on State television channels.

On the basis of what has been stated above, the main point of comparison can be the overall political background of a country. The wide constitutional powers of the President of Kazakhstan are similar to the powers of the President of France which allow him to provide general guidance in internal and external policies of the country. However, in our view, the seemingly unlimited powers of the President of France are actually restrained by practice; i.e., there are strong and independent political parties in the country which are capable of politically taking on the President or government without any fear of pressure. The presence of influential political parties and a strong independent press democracy, promote and prevent concentration of power in a few hands.

In Kazakhstan, the influence of mass media is negligible and political traditions of democracy have not yet taken shape because the political map of Kazakhstan is still rather new. That is why, the constitutional powers of the President of Kazakhstan have become almost unlimited. Absence of restraints through parliament, political parties and an independent press can lead to, and possibly leading to emergence of authoritarian tendencies.

When the constitutional setup of Kazakhstan was under way and the Constitution of 1995 was being framed, the idea of a strong Presidential system was borrowed from the French model.. However, a strong point of the successful functioning of the institution of the President in France is the fact that the powers of the President have been balanced by the presence of strong political parties, an independent press and an independent judiciary. In Kazakhstan, such elements of restraint are non-existent; these have led to a balance of power in favour of the President.

Naturally, such a complicated issue has to be approached very carefully. In our view, one of the ways for improving this difficult political situation could be political liberalization for which certain institutional reforms may be required so that the role of political parties and local self-government gets enhanced; and independent mass media is operate once on a large scale.

The basic question is not of reducing the powers of the President. What we need is strengthening the role of political parties, mass media and the judicial system so that Kazakhstan is able to develop along the path of democracy in a real sense.

NOTES AND REFERENCES

1. Baizakova K.I. Evolyutsiya konstitutsionnoi doktriny gollizma: politicheskie i vneshnepoliticheskie aspekty. – Almaty, 2004. p. 6.
2. *Ibid..*, p. 41.

3. Kazakhstan – 2030. Protsvetanie, bezopasnost i uluchshenie blagosostoyaniya vsekh kazakhstantsev//Nazarbaev N.A. Evraziiskii Soyuz: idei, praktika, perspektivy. 1994-1997. M., 1997. p. 390.

11

Central Asia: Democracy of a Different Flavour

P.L. Dash

INTRODUCTION

The socio-economic transformations in Uzbekistan in post-Soviet years are significant for a variety of reasons. First these reforms reveal the regional dynamics of transition from a centralized economy and socialist polity to a free market economy and a polity in transition with quest for systemic stability. Secondly, a comprehensive Uzbek case study of transformations helps us comprehend the political parameters of developments across Central Asia. Thirdly, political stability at whatever cost is not merely a misnomer, but a pointer to regime sustainability that has helped the country achieve success that politically posits itself where it stands today. Fourthly, amidst the prevailing regional political fluidity, Uzbekistan is the only country in Central Asia that has withstood significant political pressure, both from the US and Russia, in pursuing the reforms as it wished in order to uphold its national interests.

Uzbekistan reveals in what Thomas Friedman said about countries not changing their policies when some other country tells them they should. They tend to change the system of governance when they feel they must. For seventy long years Moscow imposed on Uzbekistan a supra-nationalism typified by this 'Soviet Man'. The Uzbek man grew under the shadow of this Soviet man, trying to create his identity. Intellectuals, who pioneered the Uzbek movements of 'Birlik' and a 'Erk' during and after *perestroika* understood native Uzbek sentiments.

President Karimov understood this unfolding political picture of his native landscape far better than did his predecessors, Nishanov and Rashidov.

However, those years were different. It was difficult to brand Soviets as colonialists. But *perestroika* blew the lid off and ushered in national pride, national heroes, national cultures and national policies. If the Soviet years were predominantly a superimposition of the centre over the periphery, the post-Soviet years had grassroots pressures on the centre to transform the politics, polity, economy and other issues affecting native national interests.

Alexander Solzhenitsyn called the Uzbeks as peripatetic nomads in the 1930s in his article "*Kak Nam Obustroit' Russiyu?* How are we to Restructure Russia?" did not strike a chord with the Uzbeks. It is rather irresponsible to call half of the current population of Central Asia living in Uzbekistan (or some 26 million people) as 'nomadic hordes', hurt their sentiments and denigrate national pride. In the 1930s, they were certainly a nation-state and not gypsies grazing cattle in mountains and valleys. This fostered unfriendliness toward millions of innocent Russians who made Uzbekistan their home for decades. The Russian left their homes lock, stock and barrel; and nothing could assuage fear of the inevitable, particularly after the incidents in the Ferghana valley in June 1989 and in Alma-Ata in December 1986. The burden on the shoulders of the new leadership to salvage the situation and convince the people that Uzbekistan continues to be multi-national, cannot be a monolithic polity and cannot give up the Soviet past while pursuing policies that address the concerns of all those who live on Uzbek territory.

THE CONTOURS OF UZBEK REFORMS

After the fall of USSR, on the throes of post-Soviet predicament, Uzbekistan, like rest of the republics of the region, began a path to reforms. As the most populous country of the region, Uzbek President Islam Karimov worked on plans to serve national interests. In his book, *Uzbekistan: Along the Road of Deepening Economic Reforms,* he drew attention to problems facing young Uzbekistan on the economic front. He listed the five principles of Uzbek economic reformations:

- Complete de-ideologization of the economy, where addressing economic problems of the society must constitute the core of economic policy.
- The State to retain its position as chief reformer of the economy in the transition period.
- Basing the process of economic reforms on a sound legal footing.
- All transition measures to address basic needs of the people and provide social protection to the people.
- Establishment of a new market economy in an orderly manner, stage by stage.[1]

Of these the priority was to provide a constitutional foundation to the gamut of reforms, ensure that peoples' rights to life and living and guarantee the safety and security of Uzbeks living within the country and outside. To achieve these goals, an effective administrative machinery is essential but Uzbekistan had only a Soviet era administration which was dysfunctional. In fact, President Karimov's intentions were clear: to make Uzbekistan self-sufficient in every respect, to raise the respectability of the State, to initiate plans for state building, and strengthen the diplomacy. He wrote several books which give his ideas on specific economic problems.[2]

It is significant that in the reforms propounded by Karimov pursuit of Western prescriptions of democracy were not automatically accepted. They need to be country-specific and in line with national interests. Western countries were taking many confusing versions of democracy at Central Asian leaders: Turkish, British, Iranian, Indian, American and Chinese. They ignored the native Uzbek model. Aware of the priorities of Uzbekistan, Karimov was clear in his approach to reforms in Uzbekistan from the beginning. He did not permit extraneous powers to meddle in Uzbek affairs. When Russia had sharp prescriptions for state building, Uzbekistan resented it. Similarly, when the United States severely criticized handling of the May 2005 Andijon events, he snubbed USA. He terminated lease of the military base for over-flights to Afghanistan.

President Karimov was clear that the new State must have a radically different administrative structure. New political institutions, a Constitution, judiciary, foreign policy and diplomacy, national security, social reforms, health, education and infrastructure, agrarian reforms to supplement the cotton monoculture and a host of similar issues were to be addressed. These required a strong leadership that Islam Karimov provided to enable a smooth transition. The reforms in Uzbekistan were also contours of the Central Asian landscape as well. As the most populous State in the region, Uzbekistan has a large role to play in regional politics.

DILEMMA OF DEMOCRACY

When new political parties are not strong enough to stand on their feet, it is not surprising that they toe the line of the President. Then, the growth of democracy is affected because of this power enjoyed by the President.

Central Asia has three clear pressure groups: i) the President and his associates cronies, comprising bureaucrats, military and police; ii) old Soviet apparatchiks, that a spent force still to be reckoned with. They do not side with the President; and, iii) millions of people who have a vague political inclination to serve their motherland.

The President is at the vertex of the triangle and, so can apply political pressure on any point in the system. The base of the triangle is formed occupied by people at one end and old apparatchiks at the other. Pro-people policies would reduce assuage pressure on the base.

Another triangle is made up of the pro-Russian elite, the pro-native nationalists and globalization gurus. Each remains pre-occupied with their agenda. The elements in the second triangle are normally watchful about the way the government conducts itself. They are also disappointed with corruption and inability of the government to meet the demands of the people.

One could observe a series of contradictory tendencies evident in the democratisation process in Central Asia in the last seventeen years. First, there is a discernible divide between the capital region and the countryside. Secondly, there is a certain degree of difference between the Soviet political system of the past and the present one. For instance, Yeltsin wanted to preserve a unified economic zone with a single defence and currency system to be overseen by the Kremlin. Central Asian leaders desired sovereignty in all spheres of governance including defence, diplomacy, economic development and social progress without Russian mediation.

Though it has been hugely difficult for leaders of Central Asia to bid adieu to Russia and embrace Western capitalism, they have preferred independence to Russian dominance. However, when the debate over a strong State versus a soft State took centre stage and it finally emerged that Central Asians preferred their native national models over others, whether they be Turkish, Chinese, Indian, American or Russian.

Countries of the region found that all countries in their neighbourhood have been undergoing economic reforms including India, China, Turkey and Russia. If these countries did not change their political system, why should Central Asian? This idea convinced the leaders and they led alike that there is no urgency for a change in political leadership. The focus of the moment should be on economic reforms.

The essence of the economic clash in all countries of Central Asia lies in the deep-rooted public sector bequeathed from the Soviet era and a fragile, nascent private sector. They were new to the laws needed to regulate private economic activities; there were no proper taxation laws to regulate profit repatriation, no knowledge of banking procedures, and no clear rules on ownership issues.

While intra-republic rivalry prevailed in drawing up regional regulations in finding for an integrated approach to the challenges of globalization, specific country rules emerged to regulate the internal and international conduct of each State.

GRASSROOT OF THE GRIEVANCES

To realize a civil society which is low in corruption, it is necessary to have an administration made up of good professionals in the civil services. All well established democracies in the world over have a good civil service system for policy implementation and a political regime change has negligible effect on it. Inputs for policy sustainability is also the responsibility of the bureaucracy.

Absence of a centralized recruitment procedure is likely to impede capacity building and breed corruption because the wrong people have occupied positions of power. Through misuse of their power, they could amass riches on every available occasion through corrupt practices. Such a scenario prevails in the Russian Federation as much as it prevails in the CIS and Central Asian countries.

The institutionalization of such a system would provide space for the public to ventilate grievances and indicate their aspirations. If it is denied in authoritarian regimes, participatory democracy would be a pipedream. Denial of this space, both political and bureaucratic, and distribution of plum posts in bureaucratic and diplomatic services by the President, single person, would aggravate the public and sow the seeds for a revolt. Applying this yardstick to the system of governance in Central Asia, it could be argued that if 140 million Muslims in India can have a successful tryst with democracy, why not the 55 million Muslims of Central Asia?

All Central Asian Presidents have a feeling that their countries need not emulate any other country. They are unique by themselves with many common characteristics depicted in the graph drawn below. All advertise the uniqueness of their national political development. All of them depict the multi-ethnic, multi-religious and multi-lingual nature of their societies as evidence of pluralism. All these Presidents do not wish to ape the Western democracy, although, willy-nilly, what they propose is democracy of a different taste devised by their presidents to perpetuate their hold over the power base and stubbornly deny any space to the people for ushering in participatory democracy. Thus democracy "by the people, for the people and of the people" remains a daydream across Central Asia. Figure 1, gives a diagram of political factors in the region.

The interlocked elements lead to mismatch of objectives with prevailing reality. While a pragmatic approach relate straight to the grassroots, a dogmatic approach would create a schism between the rulers and the ruled. None of Central Asian President is a mass leader. Although the population is small, none of them has a popular base. They have been catapulted by a quirk of kismet, to leadership. The absence of such leaders and denial of a political space to groom grassroots leadership create a glaring divide between the rulers and the ruled may further complicate creation of a civil society for years to come.

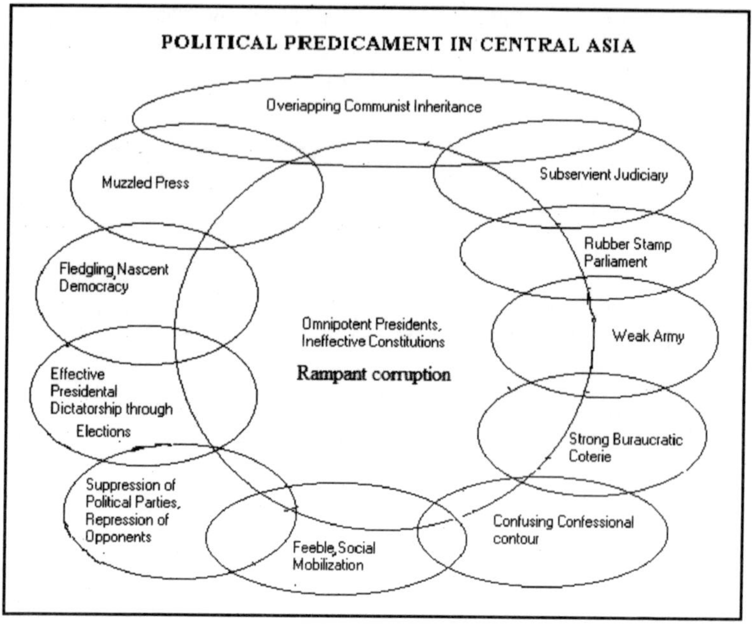

Fig. 1. Political Factors in Central Asia.

All the five Central Asian countries which transited from a stable union to an unstable commonwealth, knew the agony in the painful transition. Their leaders could not look to Russia for help to build the political institutions of an emerging civil society because Russia itself was passing through the same societal turmoil. There were many things common in their transition process as depicted in Fig. 1 above. All of them faced similar challenges in moving to a market economy from centralised socialism, and democracy in place of one-party rule.

THE BANE OF CORRUPTION

The Central Asian predicament is riddled with corruption and it is worth recalling that its Procurator General was sent to prison. Further, power sharing between the executive and judiciary is blurred and the Ms. Bibi Atazhanova was the Procurator General of Turkmenistan under President Niyazov. She enjoyed the trust of the President. Her involvement in the narcotics trade was quite shocking. It came to light only when a rival group told Niyazov about her shady deals across the porous Turkmen-Afghan borders and spread to other neighbours. Her VIP motorcade, carried narcotics wherever she went. This was happening at a time when the Turkmen state was patronizing the Taliban allowing their leaders to visit Caspian coast resorts in VIP convoys while smuggling narcotics. These Taliban leaders acted in connivance with the Procurator General in facilitating narcotics trade via Turkmenistan to Europe.

Bibi wishes to help those in power in Afghanistan. She was perhaps, unaware that Afghanistan is a disorganized and fragmented country, where warlords were drug lords. It was difficult to ignore or slight them. The differences between the two groups, like Taliban – Bibi nexus and the rival drug lord groups on the other, evidently reached President Niyazov when Russia complained that Turkmenistan was dealing with drugs at the official level. He promptly carried out an investigation through his Secret Service. The result came quick. Bibi was shunted out of her position as Procurator General and sent to prison. Her fervent pleas to Niyazov over Turkmen television were ignored.

The suspicion of Turkmenbashi was aroused over of a Bibi-Intelligence Chief nexus in the narcotics trade within and beyond Turkmenistan. Soon the axe fell on the Security and Intelligence Chief. Overnight the residence of the security chief in suburban Ashgabat looked deserted. This happened just a few days before Niyazov's death.

A SUMMER OF DISCONTENT

Corruption can trigger popular discontent. The Andijon events bear testimony to of this. Andijon, was suddenly in the limelight in the summer of 2005. Fifteen years of state-building after the Velvet revolution swept across the Soviet space, participatory democracy has remained a misnomer in Central Asia. One-man rule has become writ of the day with President Islam Karimov ruling more for the sake of stability than for promoting freedom and democracy. The brewing discontent gathered steam in the summer of 2005. What began as a protest against repression within a prison snowballed into street demonstrations in Babur Square within a day. Tactless handling which led to indiscriminate police firing, resulting in few hundred being killed and several hundreds injured. The public failed to understand the cause, the administration failed to fathom the extent of influence the "Akramia" of Akram Uldashev had on the people. The Hizb-ut-Tahrir frowned upon the methods used by President Karimov in Andijon, and the people were shocked by police brutality. In the midst of these varied reactions, the administration justified its action that prisoners cannot have the liberty to take to the streets. Still voices were raised against President Karimov in the Western world, accusing him of human rights violations. The incident impacted on US-Uzbek relations as never before. As Karimov-bashing grew loud in the US and Western media, Uzbekistan closed access the Karsi-Khanabad military base that was leased to the US. For Uzbekistan, emulating the Turkish model of state-building was dropped halfway; Uzbekistan's dalliance with Western democracy was finally abandoned after Andijon. Karimov devised for a native 'Uzbek Model' where political stability is of prime significance.

The President accused Hizb-ut-Tahrir of planning and perpetrating terrorist acts, while it propagated an Islamic Caliphate in the region through bloodless means. The police arrested 23 businessmen who followed the teachings of Uldashev outlined in his book *Path to the Faith*. Their court proceedings were over just around the time of the Andijon violence. The President and his administration blamed Akramia followers of treachery; and other Islamic fundamentalists of spreading Wahhabism. The Akramia followers said their action was a peaceful protest "to save the country from the tyranny of the existing political system". The regime accused Uldashev of being the mastermind of a conspiracy to overthrow a constitutionally elected government in Uzbekistan.[3] What intrigued the regime most was the origin of the incident inside a prison and the illegal demonstration on the streets by the prisoners. The prisoners acted hand in gloves with other segments of the society was discounted by the authorities. The repression created an wave against Karimov in the UN, the OSCE, US, EU and elsewhere. Andijon was a test of Karimov's governance and he emerged more as an authoritarian patriarch than as a democrat. His regime failed to address political aspirations of a polyphonic, multi-religious society. Thomas Friedman in his book *The World is Flat,* says "Religions are smelters and founders of imagination.

The more any religion's imagination – Hindu, Christian, Jewish, Muslim, Buddhist – is shaped in an isolated bubble or in a dark cave, the more its imagination is likely to sail off in danger....People who are feeling disconnected, for whom personal freedom and fulfilment are a utopian fantasy, are more likely to develop the imagination of 9/11."[4]

In a detailed report on the Andijon events, Shirin Akiner, who happened to be in city during the events, did not lay the entire blame on the Karimov regime. Her interviews with demonstrators – prisoners, police, prison guards, jailors, and bureaucrats revealed two fundamental elements: Both sides lived in fear of each other; and society lived in shattered hopes of building a new Uzbekistan. The protest gradually evolved; and finally when the social, religious and economic discontent fermented in the streets of Andijon, the government resorted to repression as the last recourse to put down the demonstrators. One question remains unanswered: If it is not an instigated and organized event, then why did so many prisoners, freed from jail, return to prison voluntarily?[5]

ASSESSING DEMOCRACY

In their obsession to hold onto power, Central Asian Presidents have committed a series of follies, while ushering in democracy. Firstly, none of them endeavoured to nurture the political space required for a functional, participatory democracy. These Presidents never groomed any successor or even trained a second rung in the leadership. In the absence of an effective democratic opposition, they enjoyed absolute political power with unchallenged authority.

Secondly, the closest thought that stuck many Central Asian Presidents in terms of choosing a successor was the idea of handing over power to their sons or daughters. In the aftermath of Andijon, when Uzbekistan reeled under Western sanctions and the issue of elections arose, Islam Karimov was not averse to handing over power to his daughter, Gulnara. It has also been obvious in Kazakhstan that President Nazarbaev was not opposed to handing over the reins of power to his daughter. One could well remember the main appeal made by Askar Akaev's daughter to reinstate him in power. The question that comes to mind in the context of Central Asia is: Can democracy sustain itself in the way when its Presidents groom their children for leadership?

The third is to adopt a cunning method to hold onto power by hook or by crook. Karimov was toying with that idea of passing on the Presidency to someone else close to him and who would facilitate his passage from Presidency to Prime Minister. The idea was shelved in the aftermath of Andijon. It may be noted that Karimov extended his term by two years, to 2007.[6]

Finally, the picture of democracy across Central Asia is disheartening: Year after year the same person continues in power; and term after term the same person is re-elected as President. Ouster and demise are the two incidents that marked change of guard in Kyrgyzstan and Turkmenistan. In other three Central Asian countries, old Presidents hold onto their positions with disregard to the basic tenets of democratic norms. Akaev did all that he could to remain in power, but failed. Niyazov did get endorsement of his parliament to declare himself President for Life, but he was snatched away by death. Karimov and Nazarbaev are strong presidents, who have retained power since 1991 and are not likely to leave yet unprepared to political scene soon. Both wish to propel their progeny into politics.

In this region of political fragility, Tajikistan seems to have hewn out a way to democracy and consensus. It is eleven years since Tajikistan's Rakhmanov came to power in the 1997 power sharing agreement. His fate and that of his country, hang on a compromise formulae of power sharing with other religious and regional leaders where little scope is provided to groom an offspring.[7]

This is where Central Asian countries have come along the democratic path in the last seventeen years and the future is fuzzy with regard to participatory, grassroots democracy. The classic notion of "democracy by the people, for the people and of the people" is still far from reality. Central Asian democracy is at present, democracy by the President, of the President's family and friends and for those closely associated with the President. It has not provided a political platform to groom a tangible successor to any of the existing presidencies. It has not created space for the public to vent their political feelings, fulfil their political aspirations and work out the architecture of an alternative political system that could deliver sustainable participatory democracy.

NOTES AND REFERENCES

1. Islom Karimov, Uzbekistan along the Road of Deepening Economic Reforms, Uzdatelstvo Uzbekiston, Tashkent, 1995.
2. Islom Karimov, Uzbekistan: Its Own Model of Transition to a market economy and Basic Principles of Social Political and Economic Development of Uzbekistan.
3. A.Il'hamov, "Akramia" in Uzbekistan: Extremist Movement or Forerunner of Islamic Social Democracy? Russia and the Islamic World, No.9(183),2007,pp.78-108.
4. Thomas L. Friedman, The World is Flat: The Globalized world in the Twenty First Century, Penguin Books, London, 2006, p. 565.
5. Shirin Akiner, The Act of Force in Andhizhan on 13 May,2005, Vestnik Eurazii, Acta Eurasica, Moscow, No.4(30), 2005, pp. 236-263.
6. Sanobar Shermatova, Who will be the Next President of Uzbekistan? Russia and the Islamic World, No.4 (178), 2007, pp. 72-73.
7. T.N. Nazarov, Politicheskii Dialog: Fundamental'naya Osnova Perekhoda ot Voini k Miru i Natsional'nomu Saglasiyu, in the book Mirnyi Protsess v Tajikistane – Uroki dlya Mezhdunaraodnogo Mirotvorchestvo,, Conference Proceedings, The United Nations Office, Dushanbe, 2007, pp. 14-21.

12

Political Systems of India and Kazakhstan: A Comparative Analysis

Aliya Askarovna Akataeva

India is one of the most ancient countries of the world, and its earliest settlements belong to the third millennium BC. For almost 200 years India was under the rule of British colonizers and the Indian people struggled for their independence. The most important periods of this struggle were: the Revolt of 1857-59 (the so-called Sepoy Mutiny), the movements of 1918-22, 1928-33 and of 1942 led by persons, like Mahatma Gandhi and Jawaharlal Nehru and the Sailors' Uprising of 1946. Finally, India got independence on 15 August 1947, and it was given the status of a Dominion state. In 1950, India was declared a republic. In 1947, the erstwhile Soviet Union established diplomatic relations with India.

After independence under the leadership of the Indian National Congress (hereafter the Congress Party) which came to power in 1947, important socio-economic reforms were carried out in the country to limit the ownership of land by landowners (abolition of *zamindari*), to develop the public sector in industry and economy, to increase agricultural production and to strengthen political independence.

Socio-political contradictions in India led to a division and separation of political forces, and this process also affected the Congress Party. At the same time a number of opposition parties also became active. As a result, in the 1977 General Elections for Parliament, the Congress Party was defeated after ruling the country for 30 years continuously. It handed over power to the Janata Party which was a conglomeration of opposition parties.

During the period of the new leadership, social tensions continued to increase. There was increased transgression of capitalists and big landowners on the rights of the labour. Very often there were strikes, unrests, and sharp differences among various political groups. Having lost the majority in the Lower House (Lok Sabha) the Janata Party government was defeated on 15 July 1979. An attempt was made to form a new government which proved to be unsuccessful; finally Parliament was dissolved and mid-term elections were announced.

The elections held in January 1980 brought the Congress Party back to power with a convincing victory under the leadership of Indira Gandhi. By forming a united front the Left parties of India also performed well in these elections. The Communists got the maximum number of seats in the parliament as compared with other opposition parties. This success came as a result of the work of the communists among the masses, the working class, the peasants, and other poor layers of Indian society. The government of Indira Gandhi declared that it will continue to follow the internal and foreign policies of Jawaharlal Nehru and work for implementation of the Congress Party's 20-point Programme of socio-economic measures which was started in 1975. India's foreign policy has been based on non-alignment, peaceful co-existence and cooperation with all countries. India has been consistently in pursuit of normalization of relations in South Asia. Diplomatic relations between India and Pakistan were restored in the year 1976. During 1977-79, some problems between India and Bangladesh, Sri Lanka and Nepal were resolved.

As per the Constitution of India the executive power is held by the President (who is also the Head of State), the Vice President and the Council of Ministers headed by the Prime Minister. The President is elected for a term of five years. He appoints the Prime Minister and members of the government on the recommendation of the Prime Minister. The President is the Supreme Commander of the Armed Forces of the country. The Council of Ministers headed by the Prime Minister performs executive functions on behalf of the President. Legislative power belongs to the bi-cameral parliament consisting of the Lower House called Lok Sabha and the Upper House called Rajya Sabha.

The Indian National Congress was set up in 1885, and is one of the biggest national bourgeois parties. During 1947-1977, it was the ruling party; during 1977-79 it was in the opposition; and, in January 1980, again became the ruling party when Indira Gandhi was President of the Congress Party. In January 1978, a parallel Congress Party was formed by a group of dissidents. In May 1977, the Janata Party was formed which consisted of pre-election blocks of various parties and groups like the Jana Sangh, Congress (O), Bharatiya Lok Dal, and former members of the Congress Party. The party, Lok Dal was set up in July 1979 by a group of former Janata Party members of parliament. This party represents the interests of rich and middle class farmers. The Bharatiya Janata Party was created in April 1980 by a group of members belonging to the Jana Sangh which broke away from the Janata Party.

The Communist Party of India (CPI) was set up in December 1925. At its 11th Congress in 1978, the CPI decided to launch a mass struggle for basic interests of the workers, for ideological and organizational consolidation of party workers and strengthening the role of CPI in the political life of the country. The main central publications of CPI were: the daily newspaper "Jan Yug" (in Hindi), weekly magazine "New Age" (in English) and "Hayat" (in Urdu).

The Communist Party of India (Marxist) [CPI (M)], came into being at the end of 1964. At its 10th Congress held in 1978 CPI (M) gave the slogan for consolidation of all left and democratic forces.

There are various trade unions in India which are controlled by different political parties: Indian National Trade Union Congress is affiliated to the Congress Party; All India Trade Union Congress is affiliated to CPI; Centre of Indian Trade Unions is affiliated to CPI (M); Hind Mazdoor Panchayat and Hind Mazdoor Sabha are controlled by former socialist leaders; Bharatiya Mazdoor Sangh is affiliated to the Bharatiya Janata Party. The biggest peasant organization – Kisan Sabha – is controlled by CPI. Bharatiya Khet Mazdoor Union is also controlled by CPI leaders.

India is a sovereign, socialist, secular, democratic Republic with a parliamentary system of government. It is governed in terms of the Constitution which was adopted by Constituent Assembly on 26 November 1949 and came into force on 26 January 1950. The President of India is the constitutional head of the Union. Article 74(1) of the Constitution provides that there shall be a Council of Ministers with the Prime Minister as head to aid and advise the President. The government is federal in structure with unitary features. Council of Ministers is collectively responsible to the House of the People (Lok Sabha). In states, the Governor is head of the executive. The Council of Ministers of a state is collectively responsible to the Legislative Assembly.

The Constitution distributes legislative power between Parliament and State legislatures; and, provides for vesting of residual powers in Parliament. Power to amend the Constitution also vests with Parliament. The Constitution has provisions for independence judiciary, an Auditor-General, Public Service Commissions and the Chief Election Commissioner. India comprises of 28 states and seven Union Territories. The Constitution of India provides for a single citizenship for the whole of India. Every person who is born in India or whose parents were born in India, and has been resident for not less than five years becomes a citizen of India.

The Citizenship Act, 1955 deals with acquisition, determination and termination of Indian citizenship. The State shall direct its policy in such a manner as to secure the rights of all men and women to an adequate means of livelihood, equal pay for equal work and within limits of its economic capacity and development, to make effective provisions for securing the right to work, education and public assistance. The President must be a citizen of India, not less than 35 years of age and be qualified for election as a member of the Lok Sabha. His term of office is five years and he is eligible for re-election. Vice-President is elected by members of an electoral college consisting of elected members of both Houses of Parliament and Legislative Assemblies in accordance with the system of proportional representation by means of single transferable votes. There is a Council of Ministers headed by the Prime Minister to aid and advise the President in exercise of his functions. The Council of Ministers comprises of ministers who are members of the Cabinet, Ministers of State and Deputy Ministers.

The reforms period of Kazakhstan's political system began immediately after becoming independent. The transition to democracy commenced under the difficult conditions: the country was experiencing social and economic crises industrial recession, hyperinflation (up to 3000%) and a drastic decline in living standards. The basis for a market-based economy, was non-existent.

In the wake of the USSR collapse the former Soviet states also have been experiencing aggravation of their foreign relations. There was no political pluralism, multi-party system, independent mass media, NGOs in the country. During the (1990-1993), the principal goal was to dismantle the previous political structure, the Soviet control system and the Communist Party's political monopoly. This stage saw the formation of the basics of a Parliament-President political structure. During 1995-1998, further evolution of the political structure – the core of which was the adoption through the 1995 Referendum of the new Constitution and the election of a professional bi-cameral Parliament.

Kazakhstan as per its 1995 Constitution (amended in 1998), is a democratic, secular, law-abiding, social state. Its supreme values are of the individual, his life, rights and freedoms. Kazakhstan works on public consent, political stability and economic development.

The President of Kazakhstan is the Head of State and supreme official who determines the internal and foreign policy of the state. On January 10, 1999, on an alternative process, Nursultan Nazarbayev was elected President of the Kazakhstan for a seven-year term, having received 79.78% of voter. There were 4 candidates for the Presidency. On December 4, 2005, Nazarbayev was re-elected President for the second (and last) term.

The Parliament of Kazakhstan is the supreme representative body of the Republic and carries out supreme legislative functions. It consists of two Chambers: the Senate (39 seats – where 32 seats are taken by 2 members from each electoral region and two cities and 7 members represent the President of Kazakhstan; and the *Majilis*, 77 seats of which 67 are filled on the majority system; and 10, under party lists.

Elections to the lower chamber (*Majilis*) are carried out by direct, secret, by universal suffrage and in the upper chamber (Senate) by indirect ballot. The term of the Senate is 6 years and the *Majilis*, 5 years. The last parliamentary elections to the *Majilis* of 19 September 2004, were held under the new Election Law which takes account of international and OSCE standards. The Government carries out executive authority of the Republic of Kazakhstan, heads the system of executive structures. The Chief executive of the Republic is the Prime Minister who heads the

Government of the Republic which is responsible before the President and is accountable to the Parliament. For strict observance of the Constitution, the Constitutional Council has been created.

The electoral system has been reformed. The new Election Laws signed by President Nazarbayev on 15 April 2004, have introduced unprecedented reforms in Kazakhstan. It took place after prolonged and at times dramatic public debate with the active participation of political parties and Non-Governmental Organizations. Participants in the discussions included international groups such as the Organization for Security and Cooperation in Europe (OSCE) and the US-based National Democratic Institute and International Republican Institute. The Presidential Press Office said after signing of the law: "The law is directed at further improvement of the election system, strengthening guarantees to ensure electoral rights, transparency in the election process and independence of Electoral Commissions." Under the new law, Electoral Commissions are elected by *maslikhats* (local elected assemblies) based on proposals from all political parties.

Representatives of candidates, political parties, NGOs, and foreign/international bodies and organizations have been enabled to observe the entire process from the beginning of campaigns to the end of vote count. Among many other innovations are the introduction of transparent ballot boxes and a provision electronic voting in the future.

Today, it is widely acknowledged that a lot of progress has been posted by a free and independent Kazakhstan. This has been possible due to internal political stability, continued economic and democratic reforms.

The government in India is headed by the Prime Minister who governs with his Council of Ministers which is the executive arm of the government. The President is the Head of the State. The legislature comprises Parliament with the Lok Sabha (Lower House) and Rajya Sabha (Upper House). Lok Sabha members are elected by direct ballot while Rajya Sabha members are sent by legislative assemblies of the states. The judiciary is the third arm of the government. Apart from adjudicating legal cases, it is also the guardian of Indian Constitution.

One of the common features of both States is secularism. In Kazakhstan more than 120 'ethnicities' are there. It is natural that the keywords for living peacefully are multinational and multi-confessional consensus to promote stability within the country.

As for India, it has today a number of religions. Hinduism predominates with 82 per cent of the population being Hindus. But the India's Constitution makes it clear that no religion has precedence over any other. Muslims form 12 per cent of the population, making India home to the world's second largest Muslim population. Other religious groups include Christians; followed by Sikhs, Buddhists, Jains, Parsis and Jews.

It is necessary to emphasize that both India and Kazakhstan have many similarities. Kazakhstan and India accommodate multiparty system. Kazakhstan has about 10 parties working, which have below percentage.

Table 1. Parties and Alliances in current Parliament of Kazakhstan.

Parties and Alliances	Votes	%	Seat
Fatherland (*Nur-Otan*)	5,174,1	88	98
Nationwide Social Democratic Party	271,52	4.6	0
Democratic Party of Kazakhstan Bright Path	192,15	3.2	0
Village Social Democratic Party	93,023	1.5	0
People's Communist Party of Kazakhstan	77,274	1.3	0
Party of Patriots	44,175	0.7	0
Rukhaniyat Party	24,308	0.4	0
Total			98

SUMMARY OF THE 18 AUGUST 2007 KAZAKHSTAN ASSEMBLY ELECTIONS

After gaining independence, Kazakhstan chose a new political model of development. The France state structure and Constitution of French was adopted with strong Presidential powers. This was adopted with the main difference between the Kazakh and Indian political systems.

Yet, it is important to note that both have many common approaches for development not only of political systems but domestic policy also in foreign policy aimed at peace and stability in the region and facing common challenges in international relations. Both India and Kazakhstan have chosen independent ways for development, promoting stability and enhancing security of their people. Kazakhstan and India are also cooperating in Shanghai Cooperation Organization.

NOTES AND REFERENCES

1. Ilya'Vinkovetsky, "Eurasia and its Uses: the History of An Idea and the Mental Geography of Post Soviet Space', unpublished paper presented at the 2007 Annual Soyuz Symposium on *Locating Eurasia in Post-Socialist Studies: The Geopolitics of Naming, April 27-29, 2007, Princeton University.*
2. D. Nazarbaeva, "Spetsifika I perspektivy politicheskogo razvitia Kazakhstana", *Bulletin* No 3, 2003 http://iimp.kz/index.php?action=show&art_id=150&from=5.
3. Murat T. Laumulin, *The Geopolitics of XXI Century Central Asia,* KISI: Almaty 2007.
4. A Perspective for Central Asia-India Relation: Common Ties of History. The Times of Central Asia, January 27, 2000.
5. "Kazakhstan", Worldmark Yearbook 2000, Detroit, New York. p. 1457, in Giampaolo R. Capisani. The Handbook of Central Asia, 2000. I.B. Tauris, New York. p. 8.
6. P.. Stobdan. India and Central Asia: Imperatives for Regional Cooperation in Peace and Security in Central Asia; in Jasjit Singh, Ed. Peace and Security in Central Asia. Occasional Paper Series. 2000, Institute for Defence Studies and Analyses, New Delhi. pp. 96-98.

13

Human Rights Protection in the Context of Counter-terrorist Operations in Kazakhstan

Lessya Karataeva

Protection of human rights remains a fundamental question in anti-terrorist operations at the international and national levels. Even though there is no commonly accepted definition of terrorism, there is no country or international and inter-governmental organization which would disagree with the statement that terrorism is in the quintessence a violation of human rights because it deprives people of their basic right – the right to live and respect.

The fight against terrorism is a struggle for human rights. However, this type of logic may lead to the other extremity. It is quite natural that while fighting a bigger evil that comes in the way of human rights, the State must take all possible steps to protect human rights; at the same time, it cannot be ruled out that in the course of anti-terrorist operations some other 'secondary' rights may be compromised. The fallacy of this view was pointed out by the UN Secretary-General in his Keynote Speech at the Plenary Session of the high-level international meeting "Global Strategy of Fight Against Terrorism" (2001?) which discussed issues of democracy, terrorism and security. The Secretary-General said: "The legal norms concerning human rights very well allow taking decisive measures in the fight against terrorism, even under exceptional circumstances. However, infringement of human rights does not go well with the fight against terrorism. On the other hand, it helps to promote the interests of terrorists because they get a moral advantage and they are able to give rise to tension, hatred and disbelief in government amongst those layers of population where the terrorists are able to get enough support rather quickly. Besides being a requirement of proper strategy for the fight against terrorism, protection of human rights is by itself equally important."[1]

While constituting the Counter-Terrorism Committee, the UN Security Council in Resolution of 28 September 2001 calls upon all States "to take, before granting refugee status, appropriate measures in accordance with the relevant provisions of national and international law, including international human rights standards, with the aim of ensuring that the asylum seeker has not planned terrorist acts, not facilitated and not participated in their commission."[2] The necessity of protection of human rights was further stressed in the 2003: "States must ensure that any measure taken to combat terrorism complies with all their obligations under international law and should adopt such measures in accordance with international law, in particular international human rights, refugee and humanitarian law."[3]

In his Report for the year 2004 about the activities of UN the Secretary-General put special emphasis on the following: "I once again declare my conviction that any fight against terrorism is not possible if the basic freedom and respect of human beings is infringed upon. Defeat of terrorism can be achieved only if we remain faithful to those very values which are negated by the terrorists."[4] In 2003, working in close cooperation with the Counter-Terrorism Committee, the initiative on Precautions Against Terrorism under the UN Office of Narcotics and Crimes rendered help to more than 70 countries in ratification and implementation of 12 Universal Conventions concerning the fight against terrorism and implementation of the Security Council Resolution No. 1373 (2001). After this UN General Assembly Resolutions, it has been rendering help to States on their request or on the request of the Counter-Terrorism Committee.

In 2008, the Sixtieth Anniversary of the Universal Declaration of Human Rights was celebrated. In his speech the Secretary-General emphasized the importance and efficacy of implementation of a global counter-terrorism strategy[5] which was initiated by the High-Level group in December 2004. This strategy takes into account the factors that promote terrorism and tries to strengthen the efforts of concerned countries in their fight. It establishes the supremacy of law and protection of basic human rights. Ban Ki-Moon noted that "strategic partnership between Member-States in the UN, regional and sub-regional organizations and civil society plays a decisive role in the fight against terrorism."[6]

How is the state of affairs in Kazakhstan in organization of Counter-Terrorism activities and protection of human rights?

Let us take a look at the official view point on the nature of terrorism and methods of countering it. In this connection we have to analyze two types of sources: speeches of political leaders and the norms of law.

So far as the first source is concerned, the speeches and addresses of the Head of State Nazarbaev need attention. We can draw the following conclusions from the speeches of the President:

He mentions frequently to the growth of the threat posed by terrorism, including its international manifestations. His speeches of early years of 2000 mentioned the existence of such a threat and its trans-border character.[7] In his later speeches he says: "Terrorism has become the most dangerous challenge to international security. Today the dimensions of this threat have surpassed all forecasts in this regard. The problems connected with terrorism have grown manifold."[8]

Secondly, the President has stressed that existence of different religions should not be perceived as the reason for terrorism and there is no 'Clash of Civilizations' which might lead to rise of terrorism. Terrorism grows out of poverty and human rights which, are social issues. In support, this view we can cite the following excerpts from his speeches:

> It is well-known that terrorism finds a fertile soil in unstable and poor countries. One such region is Afghanistan. All the noise that was made about the forthcoming 'Clash of Civilizations' has not come true. However, we have to bear in our minds that inter-faith tensions provide fodder to the social basis of international tension and religious extremism.[9]

> Violation of human rights, poverty and environmental degradation provide a fertile soil for expansion of ideas of terrorism.[10]

Thirdly, terrorism is not a threat confined to itself alone; it is accompanied by a number of attendant factors. "Various problems connected with terrorism have also like: conflicts arising out of nationalistic feelings, inter-ethnic and religious contradictions, organized criminal activities, drugs trafficking, illicit arms trade and siphoning off money. "Terrorism gets financial support from international drugs trafficking. At present one-third of the annual turnover of the 'Economy of Terrorism' comes from the narcotics industry."[11]

Fourthly, disagreeing with several experts activities who say that there is no terrorism or threat of terrorism in the Central Asian region, President Nazarbaev declares: "The problems of terrorism and extremism are relevant for Kazakhstan also. These problems are quite concrete and real, in the context of the globalization of international terrorism which born out of the inter-related political, social and economic problems of the region and of the international community as a whole. Presently, countering terrorism is one of our priorities for ensuring the national security of Kazakhstan."[12]

Fifthly, the President has drawn attention of the world community that this threat goes beyond national boundaries. It is necessary to have a collective system fight against terrorism. He talked about this collective system in his inaugural speech at the International Conference on Peace and Harmony on 13 February 2003, at the International Forum of Eurasian Integration in Astana, 18-19 June 2004 and in the Academy of Social Sciences of the Peoples Republic of China on 21 December 2006.[13]

Sixthly, the fight against international terrorism cannot be confined to one method whether military or political. A really effective system cannot do without unification of anti-terrorist laws globally cooperation, active in the sphere of information and technology.

Seventhly, President Nazarbaev always mentions that the work of various international organizations engaged in fighting international terrorism has proved to be effective, globally as well as regionally. In this respect the UN occupies the first place. It is the UN which would determine the principles of the struggle against international terrorism and coordinates multi-lateral efforts of the world community:

> Today, the UN is engaged in realizing the concentrated combined efforts of all the interested countries who are in search of compromise formulas with the main aim of eliminating terrorism.

As far as the legal basis for countering terrorism in Kazakhstan is concerned, there exists a large number of such: Acts, Criminal Code of Kazakhstan, Decrees, Protocols and International Treaties.

With regard to human rights it would be worthwhile to have a look at the following documents of the Republic of Kazakhstan: Act on Countering Terrorism, Act on Countering Extremism, the National Security Act, the Criminal Code, and the Act on the Migration of Populations.

While analyzing the above-mentioned documents, we have tried to concentrate on their conceptual framework and the principles and objectives of countering terrorism and extremism.

At the conceptual framework we can state the following.

Terrorism is a criminally punishable, unlawful activity or the threat to carry out such activity against physical entities and organizations with the aim of undermining social security, terrifying the people and influencing official organs of the Republic of Kazakhstan, other States and international organizations.[14]

National Security defines the protection of national interests from real and potential threats.

National Interests of the Republic of Kazakhstan imply the totality of political, economic, social and other factors of the country by fulfilling which the State can ensure the protection of the constitutional rights of its citizens, and human rights, values of Kazakhstan society and the basic institutions of the State.

Social Security means the politico-legal and spiritual-moral protection of life, health and well-being of the citizens of Kazakhstan and the values of Kazakhstan society from possible dangers and threats which are potentially harmful.[15]

Extremist Aims mean efforts at changing the Constitutional set-up by violent methods, violating the sovereignty, integrity, inviolability and inalienability of the territories of Kazakhstan, undermining national security and its defence capability, capturing power by violent methods, creation, guidance and participation in illegal militarized formations, organization of armed revolt and participation in such a revolt, fomenting social and group differences. These include:

- fomenting racial, nationalist and ethnic discord which may be connected with violence or appeal for violence (nationalist extremism); and

- fomenting religious hostility or discord which may be connected with violence or appeal for violence, and also use of any religious practice which may pose threat to security, life, health, morality or rights and freedoms of the citizens (religious extremism).[16]

The following logically based inter-dependencies come to notice when we analysis these definitions as given in the Kazakhstan legislation.

Terrorism is an act which is directed towards realization of extremist aims directed towards destroying social and national security.

The supremacy of law, equality of rights and freedoms of citizens irrespective of race, nationality, language, religion and social group are recognized as guiding principles in the legislation of Kazakhstan.

The Criminal Code of Kazakhstan has defined the types and periods of punishment for carrying out religious activities that could be qualified as terrorist. These include not only carrying out some terrorist activity; but also propagation of terrorism or incitement to carry out terrorist activity, setting up of terrorist groups, leading such a group and taking part in its activities.

Summing up, we can say that ensuring human rights and freedoms is the goal and basic principle of counter-terrorist activities in Kazakhstan.

A somewhat different picture emerges when the non-official discussions regarding protection of human rights in the context of counter-terrorist activities in Kazakhstan is analysed.

Any action taken by the Government for fighting terrorism in Kazakhstan is evaluated on the same footing as any other national approach to counter terrorism globally. The Bureau of Democratic Institutions and Human Rights in its Annual Report says:

> In some countries, the fight against terrorism and extremism is being used as an excuse for expanding the authority of rulers and limiting human rights. After 11 September 2001, all OSCE countries have taken new measures in the fight against terrorism. These security measures have the potential to threaten some of the basic rights and freedoms, including the right to live, to imposes total ban on torture, the right to proper judicial hearing,

> the right to private life, the right to freedom of association and freedom of religion or confession.[17]

As far as Kazakh model of countering terrorism is concerned, critics have emphasized that the legislative aspect is still not perfect. At the OSCE meeting on "Human Rights and the Struggle Against Terrorism", the Director of Kazakhstan's International Bureau of Human Rights and Observance of Legal Procedure, Evgenii Zhovtis drew attention to some shortcomings in the Kazakh laws which could be misused by the authorities. For example, the Act on Countering Terrorism does not clearly define concepts like "foment" and "discord", and in such cases the law would be applied in an arbitrary manner. The laws on national security mention about fixing of the responsibility in the governance, undermining national security and other acts which have not been properly formulated in legal terms. So, there is a possibility of arbitrary interpretation. The laws that are directly concerned with the structures of civil society, in particular NGOs, are also a cause of worry. Restrictions on the Activities of NGOs in Kazakhstan have been imposed in the name of national security, social order and stability. This is a matter of concern because on the pretext of fight against the threat of extremism and terrorism international standards and criteria of limitations, the principles of necessity, proportionality, etc. may not been applied.[18]

According to E. Zhovtis; "In the fight against terrorism civil society should be the subject and not its object!" The State must be an equal partner in civil society in finding for answers to the challenges of extremism and terrorism. It should not work within the framework of 'ruler and subject', considering civil society as an object of control and rule.[19]

The Act on the Struggle Against Terrorism has defines the role of elements of civil society in the following manner. It says:

> It is the duty of the citizens of Kazakhstan to immediately inform State organs directly engaged in the struggle against terrorism any information that may come to their notice about any terrorist act under preparation or which may have been carried out.

There is increased interest in Kazakhstan about human rights because Kazakhstan will become the next OSCE Chairman. But to a large extent, the people of Kazakhstan are inert with regard to human rights.

In the autumn of 2007, we carried out a survey through a questionnaire which showed that the perception of the people of Kazakhstan is stereotyped towards terrorism. We can briefly describe findings:

a. Most Kazakhs do not feel any threat of terrorism in their day-to-day life. This can be explained by the fact that within Kazakhstan no terrorist act has been officially registered. It is also interesting to note that the level of worry is lesser in the younger population. This generation is less politicised, and gets most of the information through entertainment programmes and the Internet.
b. Kazakh media projects show that terrorism is No. 1 problem of the world which means that this problem has been universalized. For Kazakhstan, it is neither localized nor regionalized. Most often cited instances of terrorism are the events of 11.09.2001, Madrid in 2004 and of Beslan in 2004. On counter-terrorism measures, Kazakh agencies have focused on the Hizb-ut-Tahrir.
c. Economic and social problems are cited as the main roots for the emergence and growth of terrorism. It has been also noted that terrorism has close ties connections with the shadow economy and corruption.
d. The State and its special agencies are perceived as the main bodies engaged in fighting terrorism at the official as well as non-official levels.

For discussing the question of protection of human rights during counter-terrorist operations in a wider social context, it is necessary that these problems are articulated not only in the political sphere but also in daily life. Absence of a feeling of threat from terrorism, dilution of the images of terrorism and counter-terrorism in information space, the high degree of confidentiality around counter-terrorist measures and weakness of civil society, are some of the factors which weaken the of protection of human rights of counter-terrorist measures.

NOTES AND REFERENCES

1. Keynote Speech at the Plenary Session of the High-Level International Meeting "Global Strategy of Fight Against Terrorism". //http://www.un.org/russian/basic/sg/messages/2005/madrid05.htm
2. Security Council Resolution No. 1373 (2001). //http://www.un.org/russian/documen/scresol/res2001/res1373.htm
3. Security Council Resolution 1456 (2003) Adopted by the Security Council at its 4688th meeting, on 20 January 2003//http://daccessdds.un.org/doc/UNDOC/GEN/N03/216/05/PDF/N0321605.pdf?OpenElement
4. Report of the Secretary General about the work of the UN. Supplement No. 1 (À/59/1) // www.un.org/russian/documen/sgreport/a-59-1/a59-1.doc
5. Report of the Secretary General about the work of the UN. (À/63/1) // http://www.un.org/russian/documen/sgreport/a-63-1/index.html
6. Ibid.
7. See, for example, Speech of the President of the Republic of Kazakhstan N.A.Nazarbaev delivered at the Inauguration of the International Conference on Peace and Harmony, 13 February 2003.
8. Speech of the President of the Republic of Kazakhstan N.A. Nazarbaev delivered at the IV Special Meeting of Counter-Terrorism Committee of the UN Security Council on 26 January 2005.
9. Speech of the President of the Republic of Kazakhstan N.A. Nazarbaev delivered at the 62nd General Assembly Session of UN on 25 September 2007.
10. Speech of the President of the Republic of Kazakhstan N.A. Nazarbaev delivered at the IV Special Meeting of Counter-Terrorism Committee of the UN Security Council on 26 January 2005.
11. Ibid.
12. Ibid.
13. Speech of the President of the Republic of Kazakhstan N.A. Nazarbaev at the inauguration of the International Conference on Peace and Harmony, 13 February 2003; Speech of the President of the Republic of Kazakhstan N.A. Nazarbaev at the International Forum of "Eurasian Integration", Astana, 18-19 June 2004, and in the Academy of Social Sciences of the Peoples Republic of China, 21 December 2006.
14. Act of the Republic of Kazakhstan On Fight Against Terrorism, dated 13.07.1999, No. 415-1. //http://www.pavlodar.com/zakon/?dok=00080&ogl=all
15. National Security Act of the Republic of Kazakhstan, dated 26.06.1998, No. 233-1. // http://www.pavlodar.com/zakon/?dok=00120&uro=08005

16. Act of the Republic of Kazakhstan On Countering Extremism, dated 18.02.2005, No. 31 // http://www.pavlodar.com/zakon/?dok
17. Human Rights. Annual Report of the Bureau of Democratic Institutions and Human Rights, 2005.
18. E. Zhovtis, Rol grazhdanskogo obshchstva i borba s terrorismom. Speech delivered at the Meeting of OSCE on Human Dimensions "Human Rights and Fight Against Terrorism", 15 June 2005, Vienna, Austria.
19. Ibid.

14

Globalisation in Central Asia with Special Reference to Kazakhstan

Kuldip Singh

The winding up of socialist systems from the erstwhile Soviet Union and East European countries was marked by emphatic claims about "end of history ... that is the end point of mankind's ideological evolution and the universalization of Western liberal democracy as the final form of human government".[1] To the protagonists of such a view the winding up of socialism indicated a victorious march of the principles of liberalism on the one hand and the poverty of the socialist model on the other.

One cannot agree with the contention that the struggle of ideologies for supremacy has ceased to exist and that capitalism has proved victorious over socialism because such a struggle has never disappeared at any point of time in human history; nor its likely to disappear in the future. However, pessimism about socialist dispensations on the one hand and some kind of liking for a Western-type market economy is quite natural in the post-Soviet countries, including the states in Central Asia. This was so because the dismantling of socialism in Soviet Union resulted from the failure to achieve what was promised, more so, in the wake of the reforms initiated by Mikhail Gorbachev. He declared from housetops that socialism was "capable of coping with the historic task of reaching heights of scientific and technological progress.... The success of *perestroika* will be final argument in the historical dispute as to which system is more consistent with the interests of the people...".[2] He declared that "we are looking within socialism, rather than outside it, for the answers to all the questions that arise...".[3] The depiction of capitalism as a system capable of curing economic ills of the world, influenced the thinking of the new ruling elites in post-Soviet Central Asia. These countries could not escape the impact of global march of capital, in which country after country demolished barriers which had halted the reach of world capital. In the globalized world, of the era there would be "no capitalism with its exploitation and oppression, its classes and class struggles, its structural defects and explosive antagonisms, making imperialism too look like a phenomenon of the past".[4]

Therefore, the Central Asian countries became receptive to advice from institutions such as the IMF that they should develop efficient market economies and integrate into the global economic system. The new ruling elites in these countries were made to believe that the world economy had grown while being closely integrated in term of trade and capital flows; and, globalisation in our times means the continuation of the same trend.[5] The only difference was that "with greater freedom of trade and investment and new breakthroughs in telecommunication and information technology markets have become much larger, more complex and more closely linked than ever before".[6] These countries were made aware of the economic gains from increased capital flows, accelerating investment and growth, creating more jobs, reducing poverty and helping them to attain human development goals. There came warnings that countries which fail to expand trade and attract foreign capital ran the risk of being marginalized in the global economic system. Therefore, the Central Asian countries were advised: to allow market forces to set prices and allocate resources so that the economy could operate efficiently; to discipline fiscal policy that kept government expenditure in line with government revenues, while providing for a satisfactory level of public investment in basic infrastructure and human capital and a social safety net; and to ensure that the private sector performed its intended role as the main engine of growth.[7] They were firmly advised to introduce transparent regulatory systems so that foreign investors would be encouraged to bring in capital, technology and skills. An effective legal system that protected intellectual property rights, provided a broad-based tax system is essential. Further, these reforms must be irreversible and stable.

Following the prescriptions of Bretton Woods institutions, the Central Asian countries (prominent among them being Kazakhstan and Kyrgystan), took measures for building market structures and institutions.[8] Uzbekistan's model of economic reforms was qualitatively different from both those of Kazakhstan and Kyrgystan. President Islam Krimov's agenda of reforms included: complete de-ideologisation of the economy; the state to be Chief Reformer in the complex transitional period; creating of a sound legal base for economic reforms; focussing on the demographic situation, wherein basic needs of the people are met; and, establishing of market structures in a phased manner, stage by stage.[9] An important feature of Uzbek model is that the government retained stakes up to 51% share in the companies.[10]

Kazakhstan quite often declared that it embarked upon the road of radical economic reforms to open up the economy and actively integrate it into the world trade system.[11] These reforms enabled government the Kazakh economy to be ahead of others in Central Asia. High growth rate and increase in the per capita GDP to more than $ 5100 in recent years are attributed to these reforms, though the boom in oil and gas prices was a major factor. The National Oil Fund rose to $ 15 billion in recent years.[12]

Implementation of market oriented structural and institutional reforms in Central Asia has been uneven and tardy. Kazakhstan and Kyrgystan have moved faster while Uzbekistan and Turkmenistan have been slow. Using widely approved indicators developed by the European Bank for Reconstruction and Development, the level of reforms in terms of prices, foreign exchange and external trade, privatisation and enterprise reforms has been high in Kazakhstan and Kyrgyz Republic.[13] Tajikistan made significant progress in price reforms, external sector reforms and privatisation. The level of reforms in Uzbekistan and Turkmenistan has been low. The transition form a state-controlled to a market economy is bound to be difficult and uncertain. Central Asian countries set foot on the unknown path of a market economy system and met many problems, the most glaring being corrupt practises at various levels of the state administration. The leadership was euphonic about reforms, little realising that the fast mode of doing business in the private sector had no place for the lethargic and cumbersome ways of doing business in a state-controlled system.[14] People used to public ownership did not easily understand the notion of private ownership and had it difficulty in accepting the credibility of banks in the private sector. Therefore, the aspiration of the Central Asian leadership to integrate their economies with the global economy clashed with the ground reality in a big way because what "was once... a closed, centralised economy based largely on inter-industry barter suddenly looked forward to play a global role...."[15]

The protagonists of reforms fee that the new post-Soviet Central Asian are not truly globalized. In their assessment, the partially globalized economies are not ideal ones for availing the full economic benefits accruing from globalisation. Such claims had been pouring in at a time when some prominent economists held the view that the contention, "openness enhancing growth and economic growth reducing poverty". Though economic development reduces poverty, it was also known that certain types of growth, particularly ones that accentuate inequality, would be undesirable.[16] Among supporters of globalization, a strong tendency was to ignore the interests of the common man while pushing for removal of barriers for trade and investment. Rosy notions, without a sound data base, have painted countries like China and India as success stories after economic reforms. For instance, it is often forgotten that FDI emerged as a major factor in PRC's economy only in the 1990s, a decade and a half after liberalization of the economy. Further, the Chinese economy has a very high rate of domestic investment of 40 per cent of the GDP as against 20 per cent in India.[17] India and China may be among the world's fastest growing economies. But they cannot be held as the most globalized economies. Tariffs still remain high and both have not adopted capital account convertibility. There are several developing economies, which are far more globalized than these two, whereas their growth performance is far below India and China.[18] Therefore, some scholars have concluded that the remarkable economic development the Asian peoples has achieved is in spite of globalization, not because of it.[19]

At the present juncture, the march of globalization has entered a new phase when critics see the retreat of globalization after its advent more than fifteen years ago. Even Bretton Woods institutions like World Bank which have been monitoring drive for globalization confess that a new phase has appeared where the main issue is how to manage globalization in the coming decades. At a time when major economies of the world are going through a recession, it would definitely be more difficult for the defenders of capitalism to convince others that cross-border economic integration is good. The World Bank made projections that world economic growth will be higher during 2006-2030 than what it was during 1980-2005 with a 3.1 per cent annual rise in the per capita income of the developing countries, halving of absolute poverty from 1.1 billion to 550 million people with income below $ 1 per day. These cannot be accepted now when indicators point to a slowdown in the global economy, a slowdown in the US and weak growth in Europe.[20] The diehard supporters of globalization may still believe that temporary set backs to globalization notwithstanding, the drive may continue because dramatic events like the demise of the Soviet Union did not left globalization. In this context, one may add that the demise of the Soviet Union signaled the crisis of socialism but not a victory of capitalism. The contemporary phase of economic recession in major economies of the world, on the contrary, indicates bad times for market-oriented economies, though the precise future cannot be predicted. Even World Bank confesses that growing inequality in and among nations, rising political tensions and increasing environmental pressure are stress factors in the contemporary global economic system.

In the present uncertain complex scenario, it would be interesting to see how Central Asian countries respond. This is a time when even the staunch defenders of a market-economy have sought a more active role for the state in bailing out crisis-ridden economies. Current indicators indicate that the Central Asian countries may look inward and would be more careful for working out the mode and terms for integrating their economies with the global economic system. Kazakhstan, the most globalized economy among the Central Asian countries, has responded to global economic slowdown on expected lines. It says that it was farsighted as the government created the National Fund for accumulating the revenue from oil and gas to work as a "financial cushion" against economic shocks from the global economic slowdown. An amount of US $ 10 billion from Fund is to be used for extending support to the financial sector to ensure the safety of bank accounts and deposits.[21] The government has taken measures like launching of the Stress Assets Fund for acquiring mortgaged properties from banks. This has injected a new liquidity and bailed out banks from possible bankruptcy. To overcome the ill effects of the world financial crisis, President Nazarbayev declared that the government would merge project financing funds and state-run national companies for creating mega-holdings to foster their national and international competitiveness. The country has taken the initiative to place all state and national company purchase orders domestically. The President underlined the necessity for purchasing products from small and middle enterprises, because it would enable them to save their firms and business make jobs secure. On an optimistic note the President declared that the country has enough resources to overcome the crisis though he lamented that times have changed today and have to work and save money. This kind of inward looking on the part of Kazakhstan is noteworthy because the country has been the most enthusiastic supporter of market economy oriented reforms. Countries like Uzbekistan and Turkmenistan have been slow starters in this regard. In the wake of the global financial slowdown, such an inward looking mindset in these countries may become more pronounced, if such the crisis persists. The drive for globalization may not be halted completely but countries would be more careful and the state would play a more significant role in the days to come. The Great Depression of the 1930s altered the global economic system in a big way bringing the Keynesian version of economic liberalism to the center-stage of economic thinking of the industrialized states of the world. The present economic slowdown may also leave a lasting mark on the economic thinking of countries. The Keynesian version of liberalized economies brought the State to center stage of economic development where the State was to come to the rescue capital in a crisis situation. Likewise, the present uncertain and complex situation may make the State more central in crisis management. In such a scenario, the Central Asian countries, like peoples elsewhere, may be more receptive to state-controlled institutions and structures in the economy. Their frustration with the State-controlled economy is well known. But the new phase of economic slowdown in the major market-oriented capitalist economies has left them confused. The likely result may be a synthesis of market and State structures, thus ensuring that globalization is not continued in the present form. The Central Asian countries have been in the transitional phase through the 1990s; this phase has continued in the 21st century. The impact of present phase of globalization would also be felt in the Central Asian countries. And even a country like Kazakhstan which has been the most vocal supporter of market economies reforms may not escape the impact of global developments. This would have far reaching implications in the political economy of Central Asia.

NOTES AND REFERENCES

1. Francis Fukuyama, "The End of History", National Interest (summer 1989), p. 4.
2. Mikhail Gorbachev, Perestroika: New Thinking for Our Country and The World (London: Fontana 1988), p. 131.
3. *Ibid.*
4. Randhir Singh, Crisis of Socialism: Notes in Defence of a Commitment (Delhi: Ajanta, 2006), pp. 684-85.
5. Michel Camdessus, "Challenges Facing the Transition Economies of Central Asia", Address at the Conference on Challenges to Economies in Transition, Bishkek, 27 May 1998, p. 2. http://www.imf.org/external/np/speeches/1998.
6. *Ibid.*, p. 3.
7. *Ibid.*
8. R.G. Gidadhubli, "Central Asian States: Transition to Market Economy" in P. L. Dash (ed.) Emerging Asia in Focus: Issues and Problems (Delhi: Academic, 2008), p. 393.
9. P.L. Dash, "Can Uzbekistan be a Role Model of Governance in Central Asia", Paper Presented at Seminar on Regional Cooperation as a Development Tool in Eurasia, organised by ICAF, New Delhi, 27-29 March 2008, p. 2.
10 Gidadhubli, n. 8.
11. Kairat Umarov, "Kazakhstan is an Idea for Regional Cooperation" in P. L. Dash, n. 8, p. 175.
12. *Ibid.*, pp. 175-76.
13. Gulshan Sachdeva, "Strengthening Economic Linkages between South and Central Asia", in Kuldip Singh (ed.) South-Central Asia: Emerging issues (Amritsar: GNDU, 2005), pp. 125-26.
14. P.L. Dash, n. 9, p. 5.
15. *Ibid.*, p. 6.
16. Pranab Bardhan, "Social Justice in the Global Economy", Economic and Political Weekly, Vol. 36, No. 5, 3-10 February 2001, p. 468.
17. Pulpare Balakrishnan, "Globalisation, Growth and Justice", Economic and Political Weekly, Vol. 38, No, 30, 26 July 2003, p. 3166.

18. *Ibid.*
19. Devendra Kaushik, "Asian Ascent: Bedrock of a new World Order", in P. L. Dash (ed.), n. 8, p. 64.
20. World Economy and Development, "Retreat or a New Wave of Globalisation", 4 February 2007. www.wdev.eu.
21. Embassy of The Republic of Kazakhstan in India, Kaẓakhstan Weekly News, Vol. 169, 28 October 2008.

15

Inter-regional Cooperation between Central Asia and South Asia: Potential and Constraints

R.G. Gidadhubli and Sanjay Deshpande

Central Asia and South Asia are two important regions of the Asian continent on either side of the Himalayan mountain range. Besides being geographically contiguous, both have strong historical, economic and cultural linkages. The Central Asian countries have become sovereign and independent states after the Soviet break-up about two decades back.

Against this background, it may be worthwhile to examine the potentialities and constraints of cooperation between Central Asia and South Asia. Emphasis is given to India on issues relating to political and economic cooperation between the two regions.

RESOURCE POTENTIAL

The Central Asian region is rich in resources, like hydrocarbon, ferrous minerals, non-ferrous minerals, precious minerals and uranium. So far as hydrocarbon resources are concerned, with new explorations and exploitation of oil and natural gas in the Caspian Sea region and other parts of these countries, Central Asia has emerged as one of the important sources of energy supplies to the world market. According to some estimates, the hydrocarbon reserves of the Central Asian region are nearly 7 billion barrels of crude oil and 300 trillion cubic feet of natural gas. In fact the engine of growth for the Central Asian States (CAS) in general and for Kazakhstan and Turkmenistan has been their abundant oil and natural gas reserves. They are major sources of hard currency earnings of these two countries. In the case of

Kazakhstan, the importance of oil and natural gas is evident from the fact that they account for about 70 per cent of total value of exports.

During the last decade and half a 'New Great Game' is being replayed in the Central Asian region by Russia on the one hand and USA and the West on the other to gain control over this huge energy resource potential of Central Asia. Some Western energy experts who were engaged in exploration and exploitation of energy resources in the region have called Turkmenistan as the Kuwait of the 21st Century. While assessments and reassessments of energy resources have been going on, leaders of the CAS are trying to adopt domestic and foreign policies to maximize their national interest on matters relating to diversification and supporting alternative pipelines for export to world markets.

The CAS are also endowed with large quantities of ferrous, non-ferrous, nuclear and precious minerals, including gold. For instance, Kazakhstan has been a major producer of many ferrous metals and was one of the major producers of steel during the Soviet era. Mittal Group is a major shareholder in this steel plant at present. It is important to note that *Kazakhmys* is the 10th largest copper producer in the world has been listed in the London Stock Exchange. Kazakhstan is also the third largest country in world uranium resources. However, it may be mentioned in this context that the CAS including Kazakhstan need to diversify their economies beyond the energy sector.

Kazakhstan has proposed to make the ferrous and non-ferrous, chemical and other sectors attractive for investment. Considering the fact that the South Asian states are deficient in hydrocarbon energy resources and are major importers of oil in the world, there is great scope for cooperation in the energy field between Central Asia and South Asia. There have been positive responses on this issue during the high level meetings of the heads of states between Central Asia and South Asia.

ECONOMIC GROWTH

The CAS have largely overcome problems of the last decade with in social and political stability and economic development. Kazakhstan has largely succeeded in this regard. It has been able to achieve sustained gross domestic product (GDP) growth rates of about 7-8 per cent during the last five years. According to official sources Turkmenistan' growth rates are even higher, above 10 per cent. Some Western experts opine that actual growth rates might be much lower than officially reported. It is commendable that in a relatively short period of time, the new President of Turkmenistan, Berdymukhmedov has been able to pull the country out of its self-imposed isolation.

Economic growth rates in other CAS, particularly in the Kyrgyz republic and Uzbekistan, are relatively less. Similarly, Tajikistan has been making efforts to overcome problems of transition to achieve modest economic growth. Despite being rich in hydro-energy, Tajikistan has been suffering from shortage of electricity. As against the potential to generate 527 billion kwh, in 2006 Tajikistan could produce only 16 billion kwh. It was reported that the lack of foreign investments has been the main cause for this situation. The seriousness of the financial problem facing the country was evident from the fact that, in 2005, Tajikistan's debt amounted to nearly $900 million and the country was finding it difficult to repay the dues. The situation became murkier when the World Bank refused to write off Tajikistan's $100 million debt.

Kazakhstan's economy is the largest among the CAS. The country has not only achieved considerable economic progress but also has good prospects of growth. President Nursultan Nazarbayev stated in 2006 that his aim is to transform Kazakhstan into one of the "50 most competitive, dynamically developing countries in the world" within a decade. He plans to achieve GDP per capita of $ 5,500 in 2008.

The government's aims is one of its "creating favourable institutional and economic conditions to raise Kazakhstan's competitiveness in the international arena". Nazarbev is keen that the country be a member of the WTO. In 2009, Kazakhstan has the opportunity to occupy the Chair of the OSCE which will enhance its standing at the global level.

CONSTRAINTS AND PROBLEMS

There are several constraints and problems in intra-regional cooperation, which affect inter-regional cooperation. Firstly, often there is a perceived gap between policy declarations and practical implementation among the CAS. Gary Litman, Vice President for

Central Europe and Eurasia in the US Chamber of Commerce has observed that governments of the CAS are after found to be going separate ways ever where they have common interest.

Secondly, the CAS were a part of the macro-economic region of USSR and their economies were closely linked. After the Soviet break-up, often there has been lack of co-operation among the CAS; intra-regional trade among them declined in the 1990's. Subsequently, there have been several instances when Tajikistan and Kyrgyzstan were not able to get deliveries of grain, oil and natural gas from Kazakhstan and Uzbekistan.

Thirdly, problems have arisen among the CAS on issues such as sharing of water resources and electric energy. Being a semi-arid region, there is great demand for water of Syr Darya and Amu Darya rivers. Uzbekistan being one of the largest and most populous states in Central Asia, has heavy consumption of water due to its rising population and high cotton production levels. Hence, it places high demand on this commodity. Being a down-stream country, it has to depend upon water released by upstream countries, namely Kyrgyz Republic and Tajikistan whose demand for water has also been rising. This has disputes. The question of sharing of water is cited as one of the destabilizing factors in Central Asia.

Fourthly, relations between the CAS are also strained over the issues of price being charged for natural gas and not adhering to supply schedules of gas and water. In December 2007, talks broke down between *Uzbektransgaz* and *Tojikgaz* since the former demanded a substantial raise in the gas supplied to Tajikistan from $ 100 to $ 185 per 1000 cubic meters, on the pretext of charging international the market price. At the same time, Uzbekistan has resisted any rise in the price for water being supplied by Tajikistan.

ADVANTAGES OF REGIONAL COOPERATION

There is a strong justification for closer economic ties between Central and South Asia as it will also bring several benefits and advantages. Firstly, experts have noted that the distance separating the land-locked Central Asian countries from seaports in South Asia is about half the distance between their capitals and the northern Baltic ports. Secondly, regional cooperation is essential to achieve market-driven revenue. This will also give the CAS more independence in their choice of economic path. The Western countries have their interest because closer economic and trade ties among the Central Asian countries and their neighbours would provide an access to larger, integrated markets.

India and other South Asian countries including Pakistan can develop a long-term partnership with the region and help the CAS to achieve their commit goals and attract foreign investment. India's public sector and private sector industrial enterprises would play a significant role by investing in sectors that have potential for export, particularly in the energy sector. There is also scope for co-operation in other sectors such as aluminum, textiles, general purpose machinery, chemicals and agricultural products.

EXPERIENCE OF REGIONAL COOPERATION

The Eurasian Economic Community (Eurasec) is a Customs Union formed by Russia, Belarus and Kazakhstan as apart of a broader integration effort. The agreement was ratified in August 2007. Bilateral basis efforts are also made by Russia to strengthen economic ties. In December 2007, a meeting of the Economic Forum set up by Russia and Turkmenistan was held in which 100 businessmen and specialists from 17 regions of Russia participated. The objective of the Forum is forge new agreements on joint ventures to increase bilateral trade and investment. During the meeting, issues relating to taxation, banking, Customs regulations were discussed. Eurasec succeeded the Central Asian Cooperation Organization (CACO) of Belarus, Kazakhstan, Kyrgyzstan, Russia, Tajikistan, and Uzbekistan in 2004.

Similarly, the experience of Central Asian Regional Economic Cooperation (CAREC) has considerable relevance for the South Asian countries. It was initiated in 1997 and has eight members-China, Afghanistan, Azerbaijan, Kazakhstan, Kyrgyzstan, Mongolia, Tajikistan and Uzbekistan. It has strong from the Asian Development Bank. Economic issues and problems are given priority in the programmes of the CAREC. It is important to note that China has been playing an active role in CAREC programmes through technical and economic co-operation. In China's 11th Five Year Plan, there is emphasis on promoting trade and economic ties with CAREC member states. Chinese authorities say that trade volume between China and CAREC member states increased by about 10-fold from US $ 1 billion in 1997 to $ 9.8 billion in 2005.

INTERNATIONAL SUPPORT FOR INTER-REGIONAL COOPERATION

International economic institutions and countries like including Russia and USA have supported closer cooperation between Central Asia and South Asia. Evan Feigenbaum, Deputy Assistant Secretary of State for South and Central Asian affairs has stated that the United States has long supported economic integration and offered its assistance as a facilitator partner. The United States provides funds for improvements in Customs and border control. According to a UN report, Central Asian nations must lower trade barriers and enable their trade regimes to be with globalization. In this context it is opined that cutting trade costs by half could increase Kazakhstan's Gross Domestic Product by 20 per cent and Kyrgyzstan's by 55 per cent over a period of 10 years.

The World Bank has strongly supported economic cooperation between Central Asia and South Asia. It has also funded some projects to promote this inter-regional cooperation. It has extended support for a leading multinational project to construct high-voltage power lines that will carry electricity from future Tajik and Kyrgyz power plants to Afghanistan and Pakistan. Subsequently, in 2006, Kyrgyzstan, Tajikistan, Afghanistan and Pakistan signed an agreement to promote this project. Tajikistan and Kyrgyz Republic are among countries with the highest hydroelectric potential in the world and could benefit from this project. In this regard, the Asian Development Bank President Haruhiko Kuroda has stated that he could envision Afghanistan as a regional hub and a critical link between the Central Asian and South Asian markets. The 'Kabul Declaration' of November 2007 is very relevant for promoting regional electricity co-operation between Central Asia and South Asia. It was proposed during the six-country meeting that an 'Electricity Charter Manual' currently being developed for oil-gas pipelines could be adopted as the basis for cross-border electricity projects.

In July 2007, the Presidents of Turkmenistan and Afghanistan affirmed their interest in expediting the construction of a gas pipeline from Turkmenistan through Afghanistan, Pakistan and then finally to India, known as the TAPI project. Turkmen Berdymukhmedov has stated that, through this pipeline, up to 30 billion cubic meters of gas can be supplied annually. This will be economically profitable and will go a long way in meeting the needs of the three South Asian countries. It was hoped that the proposal was to be submitted to the World Bank, ADB, etc. for necessary financial support. But, given the prevailing situation in Afghanistan and continuing uncertainties in India's relations with Pakistan, there are major difficulties in importing gas from Turkmenistan or Iran by pipelines across Pakistan to India.

There are many infrastructure projects undertaken in the Central Asian countries funded by international institutions and these would be scope for participation by Indian construction firms. For instance, there is a major infrastructure project for reviving and expanding the Old Silk Route connecting China and India. It is important to note that in November 2007 eight countries signed an agreement to spend $18.7 billion on roads and railways running through Central Asia. This agreement is seen as a political breakthrough in splintered region. This project proposal is important from India's perspective. Similarly in December 2007, ADB agreed to provide US $ 75.3 million for upgrading a key highway of over 1,204 km that is an integral part of a regional transport corridor across Central Asia connecting Kazakhstan in the north and Afghanistan and Turkmenistan in the South. Since these are international projects, construction firms from India and other South Asian States should explore the possibility to participate in these projects.

INDIA AND CENTRAL ASIA

India has cordial political and economic relations with all CAS and there is no conflict of interest. It is important to note that, after gaining independence, the first country which visited by the Presidents of Kazakhstan and Uzbekistan was India. In the immediate aftermath of the Soviet break-up, India was one of the first countries which extended economic assistance, in the form of credits to the CAS. Subsequently, trade agreements have been signed between India and the CAS from time to time. As a result, India has been able to make some positive presence in the CAS. India has offered facilities for training in banking and mass communications to young graduates. More than 500 young Kazak national have undergone training in Indian institutes. Hundreds of students from Uzbekistan also trained.

To promote trade and economic ties between India and the Central Asian countries, Indian firms have set up office in these countries. In Kazakhstan more than 30 Indian firms have been operating during the last 15 years. The Confederation of Indian Industries (CII) has opened its office in Kazakhstan. Moreover, 9 joint ventures have been registered in Kazakhstan with Indian partners. The Punjab National Bank has set up a branch in Almaty. In Uzbekistan, over 25 firms are operated. The majority of these firms are engaged in trading activities. Yet there are some engineering, pharmaceutical firms engaged in production activities. Reference need to be made of Mittal group which has taken over a steel plant and is operating it successfully.

The CAS have overcome initial economic constraints and are in the process of sustained development with economic diversification. Among the CAS, Kazakhstan offers a high opportunity for Indian entrepreneurs. This is mainly due to the immense raw material resources and in the country and prospects and a attractive policy for foreign investment.

India should also explore the participation of firms from Russia in joint ventures. There are opportunities in Uzbekistan and Turkmenistan which are well endowed with hydrocarbon, ferrous and non-ferrous minerals. Mention needs to be made of agricultural products (e.g., raw cotton and fruits). India's Oil and Natural Gas Corporation (ONGC) has also made efforts to participate in four of Kazakh oilfields. In Turkmenistan, a joint venture, Turkmenderman-Ajanta Pharma Limited, provides approximately half of the country's pharmaceuticals needs. India has established the Turkmen-India Industrial Training Centre to import skills in manufacturing of tools. During Tajik President Rakhmanov's visit to New Delhi in August 2006, India offered assistance for rehabilitation of the Varzob hyded plant.

India and Uzbekistan bilateral co-operation has over 35 agreements, memoranda of understanding and protocols in trade, investments, education, civil aviation, science and technology and telecommunication agriculture. But, trade turnover has been low; it was faced increasing which was about US $ 30 million in 2002.

India's trade with Central Asia has often been subject to forcible interruptions. In 2002, Pakistan closed its air space to Indian trade. Since 2004, India has made a strong bid to increase its economic activities in the region despite barriers such as restrictions on repatriation of profits in hard currency. About 30 Indo-Uzbek joint ventures have become operational and India's state owned ONGC and GAIL are being considered for gas exploration in Uzbekistan. The annual meetings of the Indo-Uzbek Inter-Governmental Commission on Trade, Economic, Scientific and Technological Cooperation should explore ways and means to boost further development of Uzbek-Indian ties.

India has to enhance its presence in Central Asia by active multilateral basis involvement. It has to consult and cooperate with major powers having an interest and a presence in Central Asia. In this connection, India should cooperate with Russia, China and some major Western countries. As far as India, Russia and China cooperation is concerned, it can be within the trilateral framework that has been put on the rails after the summit in St. Petersburg in July 2006. It can also be considered within the framework of the Shanghai Corporation Organization, particularly when India becomes a full member of SCO.

From the long-term perspective, there is a need to work for setting up an Eurasian Energy Community. India is a strategic partner of Russia and it is worth exploring whether part of India's energy requirements could be met by participating in the Russian oil and gas sector. Secondly, India could have access to Central Asia through the Chinese route; and, power grids of the region could be connected to India through the Chinese grid. Thirdly, India is negotiating with Iran and Pakistan for a gas pipeline and Russia has shown interest in this project. Fourthly, as and when the political situation in the region improves, India would be able to benefit from the Turkmenistan-Afghanistan-Pakistan-India (TAPI) gas pipeline project.

Eurasian oil and gas pipelines and power transmission lines from Central Asia to South Asia would create opportunities for trade and tourism. India needs to follow a two pronged approach in the energy sector.

India has to make significant oil and gas investments in Central Asia. It is also necessary for India to increase its leverage as a major existing consumer of energy materials. In this context, some energy experts have mentioned the benefits from an overland route between India and Central Asia is via the Xinjiang and Western Tibet regions of China. Among the various possible pipeline alignments, a route across Akasi Chin and then down the Indus Valley to Leh in Ladakh and on to Manali in Himachal Pradesh appears to be feasible.

NOTES AND REFERENCES

1. Rollie Lal, "Central Asia and its Neighbors Security and Commerce at the Crossroads", Rand Paper, Rand Santa Monica, 2006.
2. Rahul Bedi, "India and Central Asia", Frontline, Chennai, Vol.19, September 14-27, 2002.
3. Foreign Broadcast Information Service Central Eurasia (Henceforth FBIS Sov), Washington D.C., Reports 2000-2007.
4. Julie MacDonald, "The Emergence of India as a Central Asian Player", Central Asia-Caucasus Analyst, 24 May, 2000.
5. Meena Singh Roy, "India's Interests in Central Asia', Strategic Analyst, March 2001,
6. Kihore, C. Dash, 'The Challenge of Regionalism in South Asia', International politics, xxxvii, No.2, June 2001, pp. 216-217.
7. Radio Free Europe and Radio Liberty Information from the Daily Reports on Central Asia For the period 2000-August 2008
8. R.G.Gidadhubli 'Regional Co-operation in Central Asia: Performance and Prospects and Challenges' in the book edited by K.Santhanam and Bulat K. Sultanov. Enhancing the Pertnership. Published by The India-Central Asia Foundation New Delhi and Kazakhstan Institute for Strategic Studies Almaty 2006.

16

Regional Cooperation between South and Central Asia: A Critical Survey

Jyotsna Bakshi

South Asia comprises of eight SAARC (South Asian Association for Regional Co-operation) member states – Afghanistan, Bangladesh, Bhutan, India, Maldives, Nepal, Pakistan, Sri Lanka.[1] Although the geographical expanse of Central Asia would include more areas, for the purpose of the present paper, only five former Soviet Republics (Kazakhstan, Kyrgyzstan, Tajikistan, Turkmenistan and Uzbekistan) are deemed to constitute 'Central Asia'.

Afghanistan is the nodal point that connects South Asia with Central Asia. It may be noted that India, Pakistan and Afghanistan are the major players as regards South-Central Asian interactions. Other countries of South Asia like Sri Lanka and Bangladesh have been mainly trading with Central Asia in certain commodities like tea or cotton. Enhanced cooperation between South and Central Asia may benefit all the countries of the two regions and create a conducive climate for overall growth and maintenance of regional geopolitical balance. The most essential pre-requisite for South-Central Asian cooperation is abiding peace and stability in the region.

HISTORICAL ROOTS OF SOUTH-CENTRAL ASIAN INTERACTIONS

The peoples of South Asia and Central Asia have interacted, intermingled and influenced each other since the very dawn of history. The mountain barriers that separate the two regions could not become an insurmountable barrier. The powerful spiritual-cultural upsurge and intellectual ferment in one region have tended to spread over the other side of the mountainous divide. Thus,

Buddhism spread from India to Central Asia and a rich Indo-Islamic composite culture flowered in India in the medieval period because of the Central Asian connection. All the Central Asians note with pride that the founder of the Mughal dynasty of India – Babur – hailed from the Fergana Valley of Central Asia. The name of Al Beruni (11th century) from the Khorezm region of present-day Uzbekistan stands out as the most prominent Central Asian scholar of India in the medieval period.

Flourishing trade existed between the two regions since ancient times. The southern branch of the historic Silk Route that connected India with Central Asia was called the "cotton and precious goods route".[2] Indian traders lived in their own caravanserais in Bukhara and other Central Asian cities.[3] Since the Indian sub-continent succumbed to British colonialism and the Central Asian countries came under the sway of Tsarist Russia and later became a part of the Union of Soviet Socialist Republics (USSR), divergent development course and modernization processes occurred in the two regions. Nonetheless, there remains a strong cultural pull.

Four Soviet Asian republics were invited to the Asian Relations Conference in New Delhi in March-April 1947. During his first official visit to the Soviet Union in 1955, Nehru along with his daughter Indira Gandhi visited Uzbekistan and restored age-old bonds. As Indo-Soviet relations warmed up the cultural contacts were revived between India and the former Soviet Central Asian republics. Indian films and music became very popular in the region. In January 1966, Tashkent, was chosen by the Soviet leadership as the venue for a peace conference between India and Pakistan with the help of Soviet good offices.

CENTRAL ASIAN REPUBLICS AND THE COUNTRIES OF SOUTH ASIA ESTABLISH DIRECT RELATIONS

The fall of the Soviet Union and the emergence of five independent states in Central Asia provided an opportunity to establish direct diplomatic relations between the countries of South and Central Asia and renew people-to-people contacts. However, the fractured geopolitics of South Asia and Indo-Pak contradictions did have an adverse impact on regional cooperation. Continued bloodshed and turbulence in Afghanistan also obstructed a more robust South and Central Asian cooperation. At the same time, it would appear that the Central Asian States also could leverage their economic potential among the emerging markets by projecting the region as a large single market by facilitating easier and hassle-free movement of goods and people.

India and Central Asia

India and Central Asian States inherited from the former Soviet Union the legacy of friendly multi-faceted cooperation. India has extended help in the nation and state-building efforts to the newly independent states to consolidate and further strengthen their statehood. Through the ITEC (Indian Technical and Economic Cooperation) programme, India provides extensive training facilities to young professionals from Central Asian states in diverse fields. The ITEC programme also provides projects and project-related assistance through supply of equipment, consultancy services and feasibility studies. Training facilities are also extended to civil servants, diplomats and military officers of these countries. Fellowships are provided by the Indian Council for Cultural Relations to students for pursuing higher studies in Indian universities. India regards the Central Asian states as a part of its extended and strategic neighbourhood and is deeply interested in promoting friendly relations there. All the Central Asian states follow a multi-vector foreign policy, which is akin to the Indian foreign policy of non-alignment of friendship with all. However, in the absence of geographical contiguity and easy surface transport routes, India-Central Asian trade and economic cooperation would not be able to realize the full potential.

Central Asia and Pakistan

India and Pakistan moved on separate trajectories during the Cold War. Pakistan became the 'much aligned ally of the West.' Except for a brief period following the Tashkent Conference, when its relations with the former Soviet Union had somewhat improved,[4] Pakistan has remained largely an ally of the West. It turned into a frontline state and in the West's proxy war against the Soviet Union following the latter's military intervention in Afghanistan. Following the Soviet withdrawal from Afghanistan and collapse of the Soviet Union, Pakistan hoped to make far-reaching geopolitical gains in the region as a reward for its role in the Afghan war. Central Asia created great hope and enthusiasm in Pakistan for the emergence of a bloc of Muslim countries in which Pakistan hoped to become a leading member. It was also hoped that such a bloc would provide Pakistan 'strategic depth' vis-à-vis India. In July 1988, in an interview to American scholar, Selig Harrison, Gen. Zia had revealed his ambitions of having a pan-Islamic dispensation in Afghanistan and Central Asia. He said, "We have earned the right to have a very friendly regime there (in Afghanistan). We took risks as a frontline state and we won't permit it to be like it was before with Indian and Soviet influence there and claims on our territory. It will be a real Islamic State, part of a pan-Islamic revival that will one day win over the Muslims in the Soviet Union. You will see."[5] Despite the his accidental death later in that year, the quest for 'strategic depth' remained an important component of Pakistani policy vis-à-vis Afghanistan and the neighbouring region in 1990s.

The Central Asian States joined various international and regional organizations, including the Oraganization of Islamic Conference (OIC) and Economic Cooperation Organization (ECO). Turkey, Iran and Pakistan were the original members of ECO. Pakistan's importance for CARs arises from its geopolitical location. It can provide the shortest access for the landlocked CARs to the sea, via Afghanistan. However, if Pakistan had ambitions of enhanced or exclusive influence in the Central Asian region based on religious affinity and geographical proximity, it was not matched by economic, political and strategic capability. Moreover, Pakistan certainly does not appear to be an attractive socio-economic model to be emulated by the CARs. They are distinctly more modernized and have a more developed social security infrastructure than USSR or Russia. The Central Asian elites tend to look towards the West and industrially more developed countries of Asia as attractive partners. However, much as they would like to be insulated from what might appear to be the 'arc of instability and turbulence' in their south, geography and physical proximity make it extremely difficult to do so. This trend affect the stability of the region. This is particularly true about countries of Central Asia that are not rich in hydro-carbon resources like Kyrgyzstan and Tajikistan.[6]

As regards relations with South Asian countries, especially India and Pakistan, Central Asian states would not like to take sides between India and Pakistan. They have an inherent interest in improvement of relations between India and Pakistan as well as in bringing peace in war-torn Afghanistan.

ISLAMIC MILITANCY IN THE REGION

Tajik Civil War (1992-1997)

The outbreak of the civil war in Tajikistan between former ex-Communist government forces and the Islamic Renaissance Party soon after the fall of the Soviet Union aroused concern in the ruling elites in all the Central Asian states. The Islamist opposition forces in the Tajik civil war got sanctuary and support in neighbouring Afghanistan. They were also getting aid from pro-Islamic forces in Pakistan, Iran and other Muslim countries in the region.

In response to the threat from religious extremism, a collective security treaty was signed in Tashkent in May 1992 whereby Russia and other CARs provided military support to the Tajik government troops against the Islamic rebels. The Tajik civil war alerted the Central Asian elites to the threat of religious extremism and militancy. They did not want the 'Tajik Disease' to afflict their countries. Subsequently, both sides of the Tajik civil war displayed maturity and, with the help of the UN, Russian and Iranian good offices, signed the peace deal and it was agreed to give 30 per cent of government jobs to the opposition.

Pakistan's military and political help to the militant Taliban militia in Afghanistan alienated the Central Asian regimes from Islamabad. Taliban militia first appeared in Afghanistan in 1994 and took over Kabul by autumn 1996. Pakistan, Saudi Arabia and the UAE were the only three countries that recognized the hard-line Taliban government. Pakistan seemed to be pursuing a zero sum game in the region which aimed at the exclusion of India from the region. Pakistan hoped that the Taliban militia would maintain peace in war-torn Afghanistan, secure transport routes to Central Asia, and make it possible to lay gas pipelines from Central Asia across Afghanistan to Pakistan. Pakistan's broader design in the region also includes aiding cross-border terrorism in the Indian state of J&K expand view to cutting it off from India. Russia, Central Asian States and India decided to back the Northern Alliance in Afghanistan, which was resisting expansion of the Taliban militia.

IMU in Central Asia

Taliban-controlled Afghanistan became a haven for extremist and terrorist forces from all over the world, including militants from Central Asia, Chechnya, Kashmir and Xinjiang. The armed intrusion of IMU militants led by Jumma Namangani into the Ferghana Valley in 1999-2000 from bases in Afghanistan and terrorist acts in the Batken oblast of Kyrgyzstan made the threat to Central Asia from Islamic militancy both imminent and real. The stated purpose of IMU and its supporters was to establish an Islamic Caliphate in the Ferghana Valley to begin with; and from there to spread to other parts of the region.

Leaders in the Muslim-majority Central Asian countries have accepted and encouraged the social and cultural revival of Islam. But they were opposed to the political use of Islam by opponents of the regime. As the events unfolded, Central Asian elites have sought to co-opt a liberal, enlightened version of Islam, in harmony with modernization, and upholding both tolerance and pluralism. Thus, in 2007 Islamic Educational, Scientific and Cultural Organization (ISESCO) declared the city of Tashkent as the world capital of Islamic culture.

The Central Asian approach to Pakistan is ambivalent marked by a certain attraction due to historical, religious-cultural and geopolitical reasons and by considerable apprehension, because of Pakistan's role in supporting militant Taliban forces.

Religious extremism and terrorism promoted by Taliban, Al Qaeda and similar groups threaten the stability and harmony of pluralist societies in multiple ways. Terrorist violence in Kashmir has forced the minority community (Hindus) to leave their homes and the terrorist violence in other parts of India have placed a great strain on the secular fabric of the country. The world also witnessed with shock and horror the destruction by the Taliban militia of the 2000-year old Bamiyan Buddha that represented the common cultural heritage of humankind.

ALTERNATIVE SURFACE ROUTES BETWEEN SOUTH AND CENTRAL ASIA

Continued turbulence and bloodshed in Afghanistan and Pakistan's non-cooperative attitude prompted India to look for alternative routes to access Central Asia through Iran. On February 22, 1997, India, Iran and Turkmenistan signed tripartite transport corridor agreement. From the Iranian port of Bandar Abbas, the containers move across Mashhad-Sarakhs (Iran) to Tedzhen in Turkmenistan and further east across Mary and Turkmenabad (Turkmenistan) to Bukhara-Navoy-Samarkand and Tashkent in Uzbekistan; and, from there to Kazakhstan, Kyrgyzstan and to Tajikistan through the Soviet-era rail and road network.

In September 2000, India, Iran and Russia signed an agreement in September 2000 on the North-South Corridor to provide a combined sea-land-sea route from South Asia to Central Asia and Europe across Iran and the Caspian Sea. The transport link provides a boost to trade between the countries of South and Central Asia. The port of Chahbahar is being modernised with the assistance of India. India, Iran and Afghanistan signed a Memorandum of Understanding (MoU) in January 2000 to provide Afghanistan with an alternative access to the sea. Chahbahar is being connected with the southwestern Afghan city of Zaranj. India is building a 218-km road from Zaranj to Delaram called the 'Garland Highway' to provide road links to Kabul and other important cities of Afghanistan. It will reduce the time and cost for transporting goods from India to Central Asia by 10-15.

Pakistan wants to be the hub in the regional system of transport corridors. There are many tracks leading from Pakistan to Afghanistan and further to Central Asia. The following four are the major routes:

- Khunjerab Pass – Kashgar
- Chitral-Lasht (Northern Territories)–Baroghil Pass-Wakhan-Langar (in Gorno-Badakhshan province (Tajikistan)
- Peshawar – Khyber Pass (at Torkham) - Jalalabad – Kabul
- Quetta – Chaman – Bolan Pass – Kandahar

The last two routes join the Afghan 'Garland Highway' at Kabul and Kandahar, and is further connected to the Central

Asian states. The Karakoram Highway connects Pakistan across Khunjerab Pass with Kashgar in Xinjiang Uigur Autonomous Region of China.

Of late, there have been reports of China and Pakistan planning a railway link across the Khunjerab pass and a US $ 1.2 million feasibility study has been commissioned by Pakistan.[7] The Karakoram Highway also provides Central Asian countries access to Pakistan while bypassing the conflict-ridden areas of Afghanistan.

The port of Gwadar has been built with 75 % assistance from China and was inaugurated in March 2007. Pakistan is keen that the Central Asian states use this port in a big way. However, the infrastructure in the area and road links necessary for full functioning of the port have still not been developed. So, the port remains non-functional.[8] It has been reported that the port cannot become operational before 2011.[9]

The Central Asia Regional Economic Cooperation (CAREC), with help from ADB is supporting the development of transport corridor from Pakistan to China through Afghanistan and Tajikistan.[10]

However, the development of transport corridors and pipeline projects requires peace and stability, which have so far eluded the region. China can have transport corridors across Karakoram Highway and across Afghanistan to Pakistan only if these prevail in the region. Given uncertain security situation, the Gwadar port may end up as a white elephant.

SEPTEMBER 11 AND AFTER

Taliban had provided a safe haven to militants of Al Qaeda, among others. Following the September 11 attack on the World Trade Towers, the US-led military operations in Afghanistan dealt a crushing blow to the Taliban forces. Under intense US pressure, Pakistan was forced to make a policy U-turn, sever ties with Taliban and join the international community's war on terror. The remnants of Taliban and Al Qaeda are widely reported to have taken refuge in the tribal regions of Pakistan bordering on Afghanistan.

GENERAL MUSHARRAF'S DOUBLE GAME

Pakistan's military President, General Musharraf (October 1999-August 2008) promised all things to all sides and projected himself as 'indispensable' for peace and security of the country and the region. He also tried to arouse hope, with some degree of success among the Central Asians, as a 'strong leader' who could keep the militants under control and provide the Central Asian countries access to the Gwadar port. He became the darling of USA and maintained close ties with China. USA accorded to Pakistan the status of Major Non-NATO Ally (MNNA) in 2004. President Musharraf was also persuaded to enter into a composite dialogue with India. India proposed a long list of 72 Confidence Building Measures (CBMs) to improve bilateral ties. Positive initiatives like various road and rail links were taken by India and Pakistan. If the process is taken to its ripe conclusion, coupled with restoration of peace in Afghanistan, it could lead to easy and smooth flow of goods and traffic between the countries of South Asia and Central Asia across the shorter and direct route via Afghanistan and Pakistan. Trade arteries and gas pipelines between Central and South Asia could contribute to prosperity and overall development of the entire region.

However, amidst talks of international solidarity in the war against terror, part of the Pakistani security establishment under President Musharraf continued to maintain links with terrorist elements and continued to aid their anti-India and destabilizing activities in Afghanistan. The double game of Pakistan could not be hidden for long and much has been written about it in the world media. The $ 10 billion in aid received from the USA for bolstering the anti-terrorist capabilities of Pakistan were not used for the purpose and Pakistan's powerful military intelligence service continued to maintain ties with the Taliban militants.[11] Vladimir Plastun has remarked, "Pakistan cannot decide whether it wants to fight terrorism or encourage it as state policy."[12]

MAJOR POWERS AND CENTRAL-SOUTH ASIA

A multi-layered struggle is going on for influence in and access to Central Asian resources. Major powers have their own separate blue prints for promoting South-Central Asian cooperation. Russia favours a North-South corridor across Iran to be the main artery.

USA wants the transport corridors and pipeline routes to bypass Iran.

Russia favours the Iran-Pakistan-India pipeline and its gas agency, Gazprom is prepared to participate in the project (*The Hindu*, March 18, 2006). USA is opposed to the Iran-Pakistan-India pipeline and favours Turkmenistan-Afghanistan-Pakistan-India pipeline.

On the other hand, China is upgrading the strategic Karakoram Highway and linking it to the Gwadar Port. There is also talk of building a railway and an oil/gas pipeline along the route which may provide China a secure overland route for transporting oil from the Persian Gulf. Moreover, China's naval base at Gwadar provides China a strategic presence in the Gulf region.

USA wants to promote South-Central Asian cooperation in its own interest of reducing the Central Asia's dependence on the northern route. In the beginning of 2006, the Bureau of South Asian Affairs in the US State Department was expanded to include the Central Asian states.[13]

RESURGENCE OF TALIBAN AND RELIGIOUS TERRORISM

The unstable conditions in Afghanistan, the resurgence of Taliban militancy there and the growing terrorist threat emanating from the Pakistani tribal belt pose a serious security threat to the neighbours of Afghanistan, including the Central Asian republics; and, to Pakistan itself. The experiences of recent past have demonstrated that no country can win peace and stability for itself by exporting terrorism to the neighbour. In recent period, Pakistan itself has become a major victim of terrorism.

The failure of the Soviet military intervention in Afghanistan from 1979 to 1988 and, now, the increasing difficulties faced by US-led North Atlantic Treaty Organisation (NATO) forces under the International Security Assistance Force (ISAF) make it clear that no single power or power-centre can hope to pacify Afghanistan and control it to the exclusion of other actors. It is increasingly being realized that truly international efforts are needed to stabilize the region and promote regional cooperation.[14]

Taliban militants will have to be subdued, engaged, pacified and incorporated in the emerging regional system. Indeed all ethnic groups in the multi-ethnic Afghan nation have to be accommodated.

There have been reports that the Taliban leaders are trying to make use of the rivalry among major powers and play them against each other. It was reported that overtures were made by Taliban to SCO to help dislodge NATO troops from Afghanistan. However, Russians are suspicious of Taliban motives. They would prefer joint action by India, Pakistan and Afghanistan which would be supported by the international community.[15] In fact, Russia is concerned at the deteriorating security situation in Afghanistan. It has offered the use of the northern corridor for non-combat supplies to NATO forces in Afghanistan.[16]

The South and Central Asia cannot be insulated from each other. Developments in one region are bound to impact the other. During the Soviet period, only the northern direction of trade, transport and pipeline route was operative. The picture has changed after the emergence of independent states in the region. All the countries of Central Asia – despite their mutual differences in size, resource endowment or bilateral differences – agree on multi-vector foreign and economic policies.

India has stepped in as a major donor in the reconstruction of war-ravaged Afghanistan. It has already committed about $ 800 million in various projects that may help in nation, and state-building in Afghanistan. These projects cover a vast area from electricity generation and transmission, road construction and transportation, training and capacity building, information and communication, security assistance, health care to rebuilding schools. It is also of great symbolic value that India is building the new Parliament building of Afghanistan. However, while Pakistan allows the export of Afghan goods like dry fruits to India across its territory, it does not still permit the export of Indian goods to Afghanistan via its territory. Trucks carrying goods from Afghanistan have to return empty.

Significantly, some quarters are proposing that CARs should be invited as Dialogue Partners in SAARC. It is argued that, if they become Dialogue Partners or Associate Members of SAARC, it would become difficult for Pakistan to stop the movement of Central Asian goods to India, Nepal and Bangladesh through its territory and vice-versa.[17]

One hopeful sign is that, following the change of government in Pakistan after February 18, 2008 elections, leaders and officials of India and Pakistan have held several meetings. They have expressed readiness to accelerate trade and economic ties and cooperate in the fight against terrorism. The need of the hour is for a paradigm shift from competition and confrontation towards greater regional cooperation in the interest of shared peace and prosperity.

NOTES AND REFERENCES

1. Afghanistan became the eighth SAARC member in 2007.
2. Radha Raina, *Glimpses of the Past, Cultural Rhythms, India and Central Asia,* External Publicity Division, Government of India, New Delhi, 2002, p. 57.
3. For details see, (Ed.) Surendra Gopal, *India and Central Asia: Cultural, Economic and Political Links,* Shipra Publishers, Delhi 2001; Mansura Haidar, *Indo-Central Asian Relations: From Early Times to Medieval Period,* Manohar publishers, Delhi 2004; Scott Levi, *The Indian Diaspora in Central Asia and Its Trade 1550– 1900,* Leiden: Brill Academic Publishers, 2002; Claude Markovits, *The Global World of Indian Merchants, 1750-1947: Traders of Sind from Bukhara to Panama,* Cambridge University Press, 2000.
4. Jyotsna Bakshi, *Russia and India from Ideology to Geopolitics,* Dev Publications, Delhi 1999, chapters 4 and 5.
5. Selig Harrison's article in the *Washington Post,* compiled in *Afghanistan in the Mirror of the World Press* (Ministry of Foreign Affairs of the Republic of Afghanistan, Kabul 1989, p. 90).
6. Kyrgyzstan and Tajikistan are the mountainous republics of Central Asia that have a great hydroelectric potential, but are poor in hydrocarbon resources. They need massive long-term external investments for the development of their hydropower potential.
7. "China-Pakistan rail link on horizon," by Syed Fazl-e-Haider, Asia Times Online, February 24, 2007.
8. *The Nation,* August 24, 2008; *Dawn,* June 30, 2008.
9. Ibid.
10. Joshua Kucera "Central Asia: A Vision for a Regional Transport Network Takes Shape," at www.eurasianet.org, 1/14/08.
11. Ahmed Rashid, "Musharraf's double game unravels, Pakistan and terrorism," *International Herald Tribune,* August 10, 2005; Jane Perlez, "Musharraf's failed double game led to his undoing," *International Herald Tribune,* August 18, 2008; "Pakistan's double game," Editorial, *The Washington Times,* September 21, 2008.
12. Vladimir Plastun, "Central Asia in Search of Stability," *Central Asia and the Caucasus Journal of Social and Political Studies* at http://www.ca-c.org/online/2008/journal_eng/cac-02/03.shtml.
13. On February 21, Richard Boucher was sworn in as the Assistant Secretary of State for South and Central Asian Affairs, http://www.state.gov/r/pa/ei/biog/61773.htm).

14. See, for instance, http://www.sam.gov.tr/perceptions/Volume7/March-May2002/Perception_PeterTompsen.pdf.
15. Vladimir Plastun, "Central Asia in Search of Stability," no. 12.
16. Dmitry Shlapentokh, "Moscow Eyes Afghanistan in Fear," www.atimes.com, September 13, 2008.
17. Central Chronicle—Column/20080512/ May 12, 2008.

17

Recent Developments in Afghanistan and their Impact on South and Central Asia

Nivedita Das Kundu

The renewed Taliban activities in the southern Pashtun areas of Afghanistan and the increased perception that Taliban bases are serving as centers for international terrorist activity have focussed international attention on this region again. Afghanistan, located at the cross-roads of South and Central Asia while sharing its borders with three Central Asian countries on the north and Pakistan and Pak-occupied Kashmir on the South and South East, occupies a unique geo-strategic position in the region.[1] During the past several years, Afghanistan has remained turbulent and posed challenges to peace and security for its neighbours. September 11, 2001 marked a new phase in contemporary Afghanistan. Notwithstanding the reconstruction efforts in Afghanistan by the international community, Afghanistan has been witnessing continuous political instability; and, resurgence of the Taliban.

Narcotics cultivation, despite bans and eradication programmes sponsored by the UN and various international NGOs, has further aggravated the situation. The brazen April 27, 2008 attack on President Hamid Karzai and other foreign dignitaries attending the National Day parade in Kabul has clearly shown the rising growing presence of Taliban even in Kabul. Since late 2007, there has been an increase in suicide attacks inside Kabul and the neighbouring provinces. The death toll among foreign troops also peaked up since 2008[2] (Table 1).

Table 1. The death tolls among the foreign troops in Afghanistan during 2001-2008.

Year	US	Others	Total
2008	151	105	256
2007	117	115	232
2006	98	93	191
2005	99	31	130
2004	52	6	58
2003	48	9	57
2002	49	20	69
2001	12	0	12
Total	626	379	1005

Source: http://www.brusselstribunal.org/Meyer/Afghanistan0908.htm

AFGHANISTAN AND ITS NEIGHBOURS

India has been maintaining bilateral relations with Afghanistan for a long time. These ties go back to the Vedic times.[3] Indian first Prime Minister Jawaharlal Nehru said in a speech in Parliament in March 1950:

> It has been a great satisfaction to us that India-Afghanistan relationships have not only been renewed between independent India and Afghanistan but have actually progressed. And therefore, both these countries are on the friendliest terms; hence no political change can put an end to our memories and to our old links.[4]

India has played a positive role in the anti-terrorist campaign that led to the establishment of the Interim Authority in Kabul, in the negotiations that led to the arrangements signed at Bonn and in helping the Karzai government to establish stability.[5] India's policy of promoting the unity, stability and strength of Afghanistan remains firm and India has a deep interest in intensifying the aid for political and economic progress.

India's policy is based on the principle that terrorism, narcotics trade and violation of human rights are counter-productive. India is concerned that a weak Afghanistan may again come under external influence and pose serious threat to the region. It is important to ensure that, considering the difficulties the Karzai administration faces, he should be given all help to rebuild the nation.[6]

Afghanistan's importance to the Central Asian Republics (CAR) is high as it shares borders with three (Tajikistan, Turkmenistan and Uzbekistan). The CAR share close historical and cultural ties with Afghanistan. The people of Northern Afghanistan are essentially of the same ethnic stock as Central Asian Uzbeks, Tajiks and Turkmens. Thus, the ethnic, social, cultural and political relationships between the CAR and Afghanistan is deep-rooted.[7] Consequently, the two decades of crisis in Afghanistan had repercussions on the CAR too. During the Soviet period, Central Asia bore a heavy burden of causalities from the war in Afghanistan. In recent years, the IMU was provided bases, training and access to the arms market by the Taliban. The IMU, with Taliban support, carried out incursions into Uzbekistan and Kyrgyzstan. Refugees from the Afghan civil war in Tajikistan were influenced by developments in Afghanistan and tried to create problems for Tajikistan.[8] Also, much of Afghanistan's drug production flows to Europe through Central Asia.[9] All these factors propelled the CARs to play an active role in the "war against terrorism" and the fight against the Taliban in Afghanistan.

The struggle against the Soviets during the 1970s inter-twined Afghanistan and Pakistan. Many Afghan refugees have gone to Pakistani religious schools (madrassas) and came under the influence of Pakistani religious leaders, especially those associated from Jamiat-ul-Ulema. However, after the Soviet withdrawal, Islamabad sought to establish a client government in Kabul.[10] Many in Pakistan still desire Afghanistan to be a bridge due to its economic and political links with Central Asia and Caucasus.

DRUG TRADE AND ITS IMPACT ON THE REGION

The problems associated with drugs in Afghanistan have steadily worsened over the past two decades. Drug-related problems have fuelled conflict throughout the region; and it has been a significant source of funds for terrorist organisations active in Afghanistan with a global reach.[11] Afghanistan is generally regarded as the world's largest exporter of heroin (Fig. 1). There are direct links between the drugs, arms purchase and the activities of terrorists. Efforts to curb drug production and trafficking became the focus to stabilise the situation in Afghanistan.

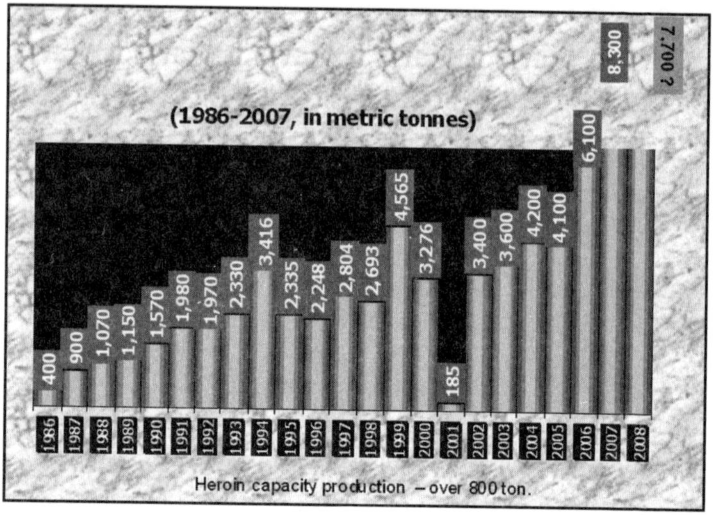

Source: UNODC Report, 2007-08

Fig. 1. Opium production in Afghanistan.

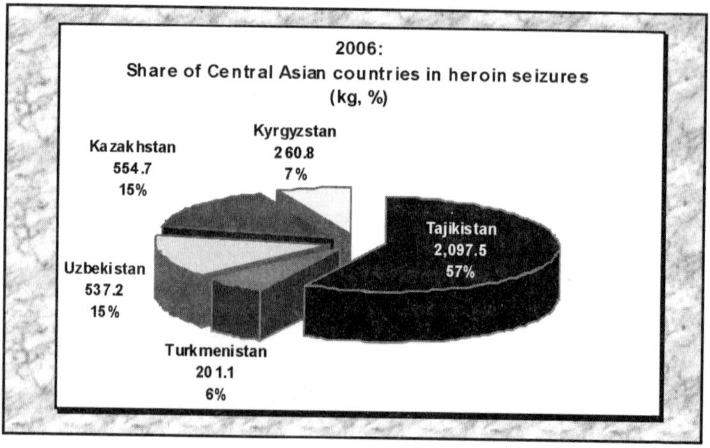

Source: UNODC Report, 2007-08

Fig. 2. Afghanistan heroin seizures in Central Asian countries.

Given CAR's proximity to Afghanistan and Pakistan and the closure to the traditional route via Balkans to Western markets, Central Asia has become the main transit region for heroin transfer from Afghanistan to markets in Russia and Europe. Though Central Asian states have tightened their borders, however, tighter border controls have hindered trade and weakened economic growth of CAR. Among the Central Asian Countries, Kyrgyzstan's location makes it geographically suitable as a transit point for smuggling Afghan and Pakistani opiates northward. During the last few years, the price of opium in Kyrgyzstan has also increased significantly. Official reports mention that there are many trafficking groups operating in Kyrgyzstan, all based in the southern city of Osh, which repackage Afghan opiates and smuggle them into the north.[12]

Illegal drugs enters Tajikistan from Afghanistan.[13] Uzbekistan is part of an attractive and increasingly important shipment route for opium and cannabis products moving from southwest Asia toward Russia and Europe.[14] Turkmenistan is used by drug traffickers as a conduit for drugs to the West, and for precursor and essential chemicals to producers in southwest Asia.[15]

Source: UNODC Report, 2007-08

Fig. 3.

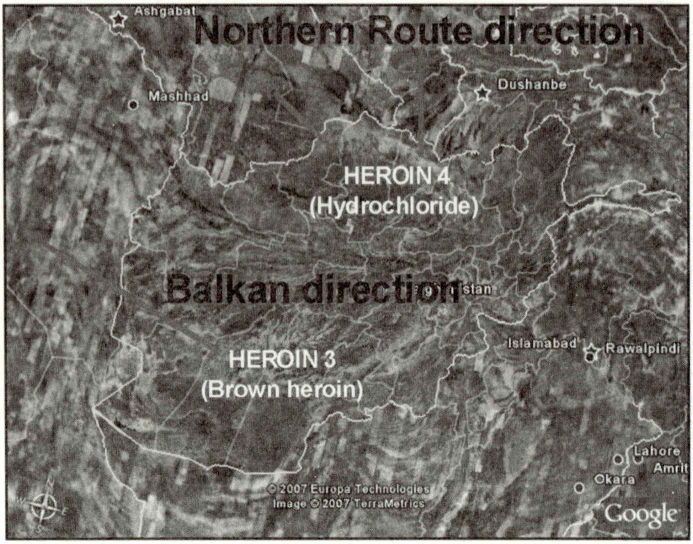

Source: UNODC Report, 2007-08

Fig. 4.

Currently, the challenge is from international drug smugglers seeking to move opium and heroin from Afghanistan to Western markets and precursor chemicals to the east. Seizure patterns indicate that drugs, mainly from Afghanistan, transit through Turkmenistan and enter markets in Russia, Turkey and Western Europe.[16] The most popular means for transporting drugs through Kazakhstan is by north-bound trains from Kazakhstan to Moscow, using adolescents and the elderly to smuggle the goods in their baggage.[17]

The drug problem throughout Afghanistan and Central Asian region can be overcome with a comprehensive development plan that should include poppy eradication, crop substitution and assistance to rural areas of Afghanistan. This plan needs to be complemented by improved interdiction, security, judicial reform and cooperation.

INDIA'S POSITION ON AFGHANISTAN

India has increased its presence in Afghanistan significantly since the fall of the Taliban structure in late 2001. It is one of the major donors for reconstruction of the country with over a billion dollars pledged for a variety of projects all over the country. Many of these projects are in the Pashtun south.[18] India is paying for the construction of a new parliament building in Kabul as part of support for the democratic process in Afghanistan. It is also building a major highway in the West, bordering Iran. An estimated 4,000 Indians are in Afghanistan working on development projects, including highways and bridges, cold storage facilities, health centers and electrical generating facilities.

However, many Indian families returned to India, mainly Sikhs and Hindus, who traditionally had been a key part of Afghanistan's urban mercantile middle class and had fled to India in the wake of the Taliban takeover. India has dispatched some 500 men from paramilitary Indo-Tibetan Border Police to guard its workers after attacks on them like the April 12, 2008 suicide bombing that killed two Indian engineers in Nimruz Province.[19]

India has a soft diplomacy advantage in Afghanistan because of the popularity of Bollywood films and music. None of its neighbours has anything comparable to compete with. The craze for Indian goods like textiles, cloths, food and art is still very high. India provides training to senior personnel of the Afghan armed forces in India. It is the largest donor for educational training and provides scholarships for hundreds of Afghan students and officials to study in India each year. India has invested significant sums in the Iranian port at Chahbahar for trade with Afghanistan and the Central Asian Republics. India is also assisting in the construction of road and rail links from Chahbahar to the Iranian border with Afghanistan and the Central Asian Republics. This investment is necessary because of Pakistan's refusal to permit India cross-shipment rights across Pakistan to Afghanistan and beyond.[20]

India has a multi-dimensional cooperation programme with Afghanistan and is committed to pursue these on a quick-delivery, cost-effective basis.[21] India is also trying to accelerate work on the Turkmenistan-Afghanistan-Pakistan-India (TAPI) gas pipeline project. Afghanistan is also showing keen interest in the project and its government even adopted a declaration emphasising how Afghanistan could become an "energy bridge" through the TAPI gas pipeline.[22] However, the objective of Taliban is to see that India withdraws from developmental activities in Afghanistan. India refuses to succumb to these pressures from such forces.

India's non-participation in military operations along with multinational forces has helped India to retain the image of a genuine ally among the Afghan people. Afghan government has been keen on India playing a greater role in training the Afghan National Security Forces.[23] The very fact that the Indian diplomatic mission in Kabul continued to function while various Afghan factions incessantly bombarded the city, is testimony to the significance of Afghanistan for India. India again displayed the same determination when the Indian Embassy in Kabul was made operational within days of the July 7, 2008 attack in which senior Indian officials, including the defense attaché, were killed.[24] Continued Pakistani ambivalence toward the Taliban might be due to Pakistan's concern that India is trying to encircle it by gaining influence in Afghanistan. Pakistan's security officials might feel that the Taliban offers the best chance of countering India's growing regional influence. Pakistan also believes that ethnic Tajiks and other ethnic constituents of the former Northern Alliance in Afghanistan that opposed the largely Pashtun Taliban prior to 9/11 receive support from India and that India foments separatism in Pakistan's restive Baluchistan province from its consulates in Afghanistan.[25] However, in spite of the diverse agendas of various actors in the Afghan conflict, India will maintain its strong presence in Afghanistan and review of politics in and around Afghanistan.

FUTURE OPTIONS

As far as action on India's part is concerned, the following may be mentioned:

- There is a need for stronger regional initiative to help stabilize Afghanistan.
- There is a need to implement a strong strategy to tame the Taliban.
- Regional groupings could make a coordinated effort to assist Afghanistan in capacity building, human resource development, building Institutions of governance and critical infrastructure.

CONCLUSION

The resurgence of Taliban in Afghanistan has a negative impact on the political and economic development of Afghanistan. There is a need for cooperation from all countries of the region to end terrorism in Afghanistan. Hence, transforming regional security perceptions among the Afghans, Central Asians, Pakistanis and Indians will be a monumental challenge. But it could constitute a major way to stabilise and secure Afghanistan.

NOTES AND REFERENCES

1. "Afghanistan Factor in Central and South Asian Politics", Himalayan Research and Cultural Foundation, available at *http://www.kashmir-information.com/Afghanistan/index.html,* accessed on 05th, November, 2008.
2. Mark John and Paul Taylor, "NATO says near deal on Russian Afghan help", Afhgan News, March 15, 2008 available at http://www.afghanistannewscenter.com/news/2008/march/mar152008.html, accessed on 05th November, 2008.
3. Khosla I.P., "Indo-Afghan Relations: Looking into the Future", in Shreedhar ed.*Afghanistan in Transition*, Indian Council of World Affairs, New Delhi, 2003, pp. 117.
4. *Ibid.*
5. *Ibid.*
6. Jayshree Bajoria, *India-Afghanistan Relations*, October 23, 2008, Council Foreign Relations, available at http://www.cfr.org/publication/17474/indiaafghanistan_relations.html, accessed on 6th Nov. 2008.
7. Mann Poonam, "Role of Neighbours: Central Asian Republics", in Shreedhar ed.*Afghanistan in Transition*, Indian Council of World Affairs, New Delhi, 2003, pp. 62-64.
8. Oscar Schlyter, "Impact of the Taliban Regime, on Security in the Central Asian Region", in Inglof Kiesow ed., From *Taiwan to Taliban*, Swedish Defence Research Agency, Stockholm, February 2002,p.256.
9. Glenn W. Goodman, "Central Asian Patterns: Low Key Spadework's, Valuable Benefits for War in Afghanistan", Armed Forces Journal, January 2002, p. 60.
10. Pattanaik S. Smruti, "Pakistan and the New Regime in Afghanistan: Relationship at Crossroads", in Shreedhar ed.*Afghanistan in Transition*, Indian Council of World Affairs, New Delhi, 2003, pp. 75-77.
11. Chossudovsky Michel, "The Spoils of War: Afghanistan's Multibillion Dollar Heroin Trade", 5th April 2004, available at http://globalresearch.ca/articles/CHO404A.html.
12. Kate Heiska, "OSCE Border Management Activities in Central Asia and Prospect for Cooperation with Afghanistan", OSCE Project Report, 2007-08.
13. Lawrence W.E.,"Border Management Project for Badahkshan Afghanistan", BOMBAF, UNDP Project Report, July 2008.

14. Brannerud Christer,"Opiate Situation: Hypothesis, Theories and Speculations",UNODC Project Report, June 2008.
15. *Ibid.*
16. *Ibid.*
17. Raphael F. Perl,*Taliban and the Drug Trade*, CRS Report for Congress, Code RS21041 October 5, 2001.
18. *Ibid.*
19. Mariet D'Souza Shanthie, "Should India Continue its Present Course in Afghanistan"? *IDSA Strategic Comment*, Institute for Defence Studies and Analyses, New Delhi, July 09, 2008.
20. Tharoor Shashi,Making the Most of India's Soft Power, *The Times of India, January 28, 2007.*
21. Sahgal Arun, Anand V.K.,"Post-Kabul Attack, India Needs to be More Assertive in Afghanistan,"16 July 2008 , Available at http://www.nerve.in/news., accessed on 15th November 2008.
22. Turkmenistan looks at TAPI Project, *Turkmenistan New Eurasia*, available at http://turkmenistan.neweurasia.net/2008/04/30/turkmenistan-looks-at-tapi-project/
23. *Ibid.*
24. *Ibid.*
25. Chandra Vishal, "The July 7 Attack in Kabul and India's Search for a Response", *IDSA Strategic Comment*, Institute for Defence Studies and Analyses, New Delhi, July 18, 2008.

Annexure I

The India-Central Asia Foundation (ICAF)

GENERAL INFORMATION

The India – Central Asia Foundation (ICAF) was established as a registered society in Delhi on March 1, 2005. ICAF is governed by a Governing Body (GB) whose members are distinguished personalities from various walks of life. The current President and Vice-President is Shri K. Santhanam, distinguished scientist and Shri K. Raghunath, former foreign secretary of India respectively. At present, Prof. Nirmala Joshi is the Director and Dr. Ramakant Dwivedi is the Research Coordinator.

It is now increasingly recognized that the importance of Central Asia to India is multi-spectral: civilisational, historical, geopolitical and economic. And, the area invites fresh and focused studies to advance common interests and concerns.

It is emerging as an area rich in strategic, economic and trade terms. Its historical and cultural linkages with India would, of course, continue to be of abiding interest. But awareness of and sensitivity to contemporary events in Central Asia are of higher importance in promoting common interests.

These countries, uniformly, display unique warmth towards India and a desire for a significant increase in bilateral interactions. In their perception, India is a welcome and benign neighbour. These countries also have a desire to learn from India's developmental experience in pluralist politics and post-1991 economics.

India's interests in Central Asia deserve to be effectively advanced by diversifying from cooperation in education and culture to high technology interactions and enhanced business transactions. And, there is a firm need to provide professional and timely research advisories for Indian and Central Asian entrepreneurs on the new pathways and markets in Central Asia, Eurasia and the world at large.

OBJECTIVES

The India Central Asia Foundation is a Track-II non-profit organisation based in Delhi whose objectives would include the following:

a) creation of an institutional framework in which the links between India and Central Asia are strengthened in sectors of activities like the political, economic, strategic, military, science & technology and cultural;
b) extension of the above concept in respect of Eurasia;
c) creation and maintenance of a data bank in India to generate and provide information of relevance to scholars, entrepreneurs, technocrats, scientists and other professionals in India and Central Asia for enhancing bilateral and multi-lateral interactions;
d) promotion of scholarly exchanges in Indian and Central Asian Studies between appropriate institutions;
e) conduct of periodic seminars, workshops and conferences;
f) publications to advance the aims and objectives of the society; and,
g) raising, management and application of funds to advance the objectives of the society.

GOVERNANCE

The Governing Body of the Foundation for the period 2008-2011 is composed of the following Founding Members:

• Shri K. Santhanam Distinguished Scientist	President
• Shri K. Raghunath Former Foreign Secretary	Vice President
• Prof. Nirmala Joshi Former Professor, JNU	Director

- Dr. Ramakant Dwivedi — Member
  Strategic Analyst
- Dr. B.B. Kumar — Member
  Educationist
- Prof. R.G. Gidadhubli — Member
  Economist
- Dr. Gulshan Sachdeva — Member
  Associate Professor JNU
- Shri J.N. Roy — Member
  Retd IPS Officer
- Shri Rajesh Bhargava — Member
  Engineer
- Brig (Retd) Devinder Singh — Member
  Defence Analyst
- Mrs Sudha Mahalingam — Member
  Energy Expert

BILATERAL AND MULTILATERAL INTERACTIONS

The ICAF has bilateral ties with the following Institutes, Universities and Centres:

- Centre for Strategic Research under the President of the Republic of Tajikistan, Dushanbe, Tajikistan
- Research Centre Sharq, Dushanbe, Tajikistan
- Institute of Oriental Studies, Ministry of Education and Sciences, Almaty, Kazakhstan
- The Foundation of Regional Policy, Tashkent, Uzbekistan
- Kazakhstan Institute for Strategic Studies, Kazakhstan
- Department of International Relations and Foreign Policy, Al-Farabi Kazakh National University, Almaty, Kazakhstan
- Centre for Political Studies, Tashkent, Uzbekistan
- Institute for Strategic and Regional Studies, Tashkent, Uzbekistan
- Russian Institute for Strategic Studies, Moscow, Russia
- Diplomatic Academy, Bishkek, Kyrgyz Republic
- Institute of History under the President of the Republic of Turkmenistan, Ashgabat

VISITING SCHOLARS

The ICAF offers research facilities for foreign research scholars/ students. Those who wish to join ICAF as Visiting Fellows may contact the ICAF office.

For more details, contact:

The India-Central Asia Foundation
S – 523 A, Greater Kailash II, New Delhi – 110048

And

C 9/ 9872, Vasant Kunj, New Delhi - 110 070
Tel: 91-11- 26136739 Fax: 91-11-26136739
E-mail: icafindia@gmail.com

Annexure II

Al-Farabi Kazakh National University

Al-Farabi Kazakh National University is the leading higher educational institution of the Republic of Kazakhstan. Based in 1934, it has passed the big and difficult way, having made great contribution to the development of native science, technique, culture, and higher education.

Al-Farabi KazNU first among the institutes of higher education of Kazakhstan and Central Asia have signed the Magna Charta Universitatum and was included to the European education space, having proclaimed as its goal the attainment of Europeans standards – fundamental and recognized education at an international level and the highly competitive graduates at the world labour market. At present KazNU successfully cooperating with more than 400 largest universities of the world, is member of International Association of Universities.

KazNU's multilevel education system includes: higher basic education (bachelor degree), higher special education, magistracy, post-graduate education, doctorate. Admission to KazNU is realized by the state educational grants and credits, and on contract base. Specialists have been training in more than 180 specialties. Today Al-Farabi KazNU has 14 faculties, college, institute of Professional Development, 7 scientific-research institutes, 25 specialized boards on defense of doctoral thesis in 67 specialties, more than 15 thousand students, MA students and PhD students. Scientific infrastructure of the university also includes 11centers. More than 2000 teachers and employers including 6 academics, ISA HS, 27 academics of NSA Republic of Kazakhstan, 21 honoured worker of the Republic of Kazakhstan, 24 laureates of the state and nominal premium of the Republic of Kazakhstan, 39 laureates of young scientist's premium, 300 professors, doctors of science, and more than 800 assistant of professors, candidates of science are working at 101 departments.

14 DEPARTMENTS WITH 105 CHAIRS

- Mechanics & Mathematics
- Geography
- Philosophy and Political Studies
- Economics & Business
- Law
- Oriental Studies
- International Relations
- Physics
- Biology
- Chemistry
- Language Studies
- Journalism
- History
- Intensive Pre-Training for Foreign Students

Professional Development Institute
Computer-Center
University incorporates:

7 RESEARCH INSTITUTES AND "TECHNOPARK"

- RI for Experimental and Theoretical Physics
- Combustion Problems Institute
- RI for New Chemical Technologies and Materials
- RI of Biology and Biotechnology
- RI of Ecology
- RI of Mathematics and Mechanics
- Center for Physical and Chemical Methods of Analysis

Scientific-Technological Park

SCIENTIFIC CENTERS:

- Chinese Language
- Kazakhstan-India Center of Information Technologies
- al-Farabi Center

- Ancient Turkic Manuscripts
- Economic and Mathematic Research
- Historic Research
- Tourism
- Political and Electoral Technologies
- Ethnic Psychology and Pedagogics
- European Documentation
- Experimental Center

PROSPECTS FOR COOPERATION WITH FOREIGN UNIVERSITIES

- Joint Ph.D. programmes
- Student & Faculty exchange
- Joint research projects
- Joint events (conferences, workshops, exhibitions, etc.)
- Joint publishing of books and other training materials

Annexure III

Faculty of International Relations, Al-Farabi Kazakh National University

Faculty of International Relations of Al-Farabi Kazakh National University is one of the leading faculties of Kazakhstan in this field. The Faculty was set up during the difficult period when Kazakhstan was taking shape as an independent State. The Faculty of International Relations came into existence in the year 1995 as per the decision of the Academic Council of the University and on the request of the Ministry of Foreign Affairs of the Republic of Kazakhstan.

The Faculty of International Relations has now become a major centre of education and research, and it is making significant contribution in preparing highly qualified specialists. The Faculty prepares highly competitive experts in international relations, international law and area studies at B.A. and M.A. levels. In the year 2005 Ph.D. programme was also started in the Faculty on experimental basis as a project of the Ministry of Education and Science of Kazakhstan.

The Faculty has 5 Departments: Department of International Relations and Foreign Policy of the Republic of Kazakhstan, Department of International Law, Department of World Economy, Department of Modern Oriental Languages, and Department of Foreign Languages. Quality of teaching and research is maintained by 125 highly qualified faculty members having D.Litt and Ph.D. in their field. The Faculty has amongst its staff Professors, Readers, practicing specialists with experience of work in the Ministry of

Foreign Affairs of Kazakhstan, as well as experience of teaching and research. Most of the faculty members have undergone higher training in foreign universities.

The Faculty is carrying out its work in close cooperation with foreign embassies, foreign representatives and companies, and cultural centres of the embassies. Representatives of embassies, diplomats, as also representatives of international organizations, like UN, European Union, OSCE, Goethe Institute, DAAD, USIS, British Council, and French Centre are invited to deliver public lectures in the Faculty.

The main thrust of research of the Faculty of International Relations is in the following areas:

1. Main trends of the foreign policy of Kazakhstan, bilateral and multilateral relations;
2. Problems of European integration;
3. Contemporary issues in international relations;
4. Asian direction including regional problems, issues of cooperation of the countries of Central Asia with India, China and other countries of the region;
5. Problems of integration processes in relation to international law in the post-Soviet space; contemporary problems of international law;
6. System of national interests of Kazakhstan and priorities of national security in relation to globalization;
7. Role of foreign languages in relation to integration process and globalization.

Research work in the Faculty is carried out in various ways: D.Litt. and Ph.D. programmes; publication of monographs; collections of research articles; collections of foreign policy documents; conference papers; publication of materials of international and regional conferences, round tables, seminars, students' research activities. The results of research are included in the teaching process.

The Faculty publishes a bimonthly research journal *Vestnik KazNU. Series: International Relations and International Law,* edited by K.I.Baizakova, D.Litt., Professor and Dean of the Faculty.

RESEARCH CENTRES

In the year 1998 a Centre for European Documentation (CED) was set up which has got the status of FULL EDC. As per this grant CED is regularly receiving different documents directly from the Information Centre in Brussels and Luxemburg. CED organizes conferences, seminars, round tables on problems of European integration for the benefit of future specialists in international studies and area studies. CED is also regularly publishing an informative and analytical journal *European Dialogue*.

In the year 2003 a **Resource Centre for American and Democratic Studies** (RCADS) was set up within the Faculty under the Programme of Cooperation with the New School University, New York, USA. The Centre's library of 6000 titles consists of printed and electronic material. Students of various categories doing M.A., Ph.D. and D.Litt are given access to these documents and material on the history, theory, foreign policy, and political system of USA which they can use to prepare for seminars, for writing term papers, dissertations, Ph.D. and D.Litt theses.

In the year 2006 a **NATO Information Centre** was set up under the Programme of Cooperation with the Department of Social Diplomacy of NATO. This Information Centre has been provided with literature, audio and video material on various problems of NATO, and it is proving to be of immense help in teaching and research.

It is expected that a **Resource Centre for Regional Studies of Asia** (RCRSA) will come into being in the year 2006. This Centre will be provided with literature by the research centres of Asian countries. Cooperation within the framework of RCRSA will help to develop specializatiions on India, China, Japan and other Asian countries.

International collaboration of the Faculty with leading foreign universities is aimed at training a new generation of specialists in international relations taking into consideration the latest positive experience of foreign specialists and centres engaged in the training of such specialists, using suitable methods, and holding regular consultations with experts from the countries of Europe, America and Asia.

Since 1997 the Faculty of International Relations has a Research Council which deals with the matters relating to Ph.D. and D.Litt theses on the specialization no. 07.00.15 – 'History of International Relations and Foreign Policy'. Well-known Kazakh diplomats have defended their work before this Research Council and got their Ph.D. / D.Litt. degrees. Amongst such diplomats are: K.K.Tokaev (Minister of Foreign Affairs), A.A.Musinov (Ambassador of the Republic of Kazakhstan to Saudi Arabia), D.T.Zhakenov (Head of the Department of Protocol, Ministry of Foreign Affairs, Almaty, Kazakhstan).

Annexure IV

Indian Council of World Affairs
Sapru House, Barakhamba Road, New Delhi

The Indian Council of World Affairs (ICWA) was established in 1943 under the Registration of Societies Act 1860 as a non-political organization for the study of international relations. In 2001, the ICWA was constituted as a body corporate by an Act of Parliament and was accorded the status of an Institute of National importance.

ICWA is geared towards promotion of study of Indian and International affairs so as to develop a body of informed opinion on international matters. The institute endeavours to promote India's relations with other countries through study, research, discussions, lectures, exchange of ideas and information with other organizations within and outside India engaged in similar activities and serves as a clearing house of information and knowledge regarding world affairs.

To achieve the objectives, ICWA is engaged in publishing books, periodicals, journals, reviews, papers, pamphlets and other literature, establishes contacts with organizations dealings with subjects of interest of ICWA, arranges conferences and seminars and undertakes any such activity which promotes the ideas and objectives of ICWA.

The Indian Council of World Affairs publishes 'India Quarterly', a journal on international affairs. This was started in 1945 and has an unbroken record of publication. In 2009 it entered into 65th year of its publication.

The Indian Council of World Affairs has a 47 member Council headed by Hon'ble Vice President of India, Shri Mohammad Hamid Ansari. The three Vice Presidents of the Council are Shri Pranab

Mukherjee, Hon'ble Minister for External Affairs and Finance, Government of India, Dr. Laxminarayan Pandey, Hon'ble Member of Parliament and Shri Jagmohan, former Cabinet Minister. The Chief Executive Officer of ICWA is Ambassador Ashok Kumar, Additional Secretary, Ministry of External Affairs and Acting Director General of ICWA.

Index